THE SEASONS PLATE COOKBOOK

CELEBRATING 10 YEARS OF SEASONS PLATE LUNCHES AT WYNDHAM ESTATE

THE SEASONS PLATE COOKBOOK

CELEBRATING 10 YEARS OF SEASONS PLATE LUNCHES AT WYNDHAM ESTATE

Edited by Lucy Malouf
Photography by Adrian Lander

Hardie Grant Books

THE SEASONS PLATE COOKBOOK
Published by Hardie Grant Publishing Pty Ltd
for Wyndham Estate
700 Dalwood Rd
Dalwood NSW Australia 2335
www.wyndhamestate.com.au

Hardie Grant Publishing
12 Claremont Street
South Yarra VIC 3141
Australia
www.hardiegrant.com.au

All rights reserved. No part of this publication may be reproduced, stored in a retrieval system or transmitted in any form by any means, electronic, mechanical, photocopying, recording, or otherwise, without prior written permission of the publishers and copyright holders.

Copyright © 2004 Orlando Wyndham Group Pty Ltd
(ABN 75 007 070 046)

Editor, Lucy Malouf
Design, Klarissa Pfisterer Design
Photography, Adrian Lander
Food Styling, Opel Khan
Pre-press, DIG
Printing, Tien Wah Press
National Library of Australia
cataloguing-in-publication data:

Seasons plate cookbook.
Includes index.
ISBN 1 74066 191 5.
1. Cookery. I. Malouf, Lucy.
II. Wyndham Estate Wines Limited.
641.5

Introduction

Wyndham Estate is one of Australia's most enduring and popular wineries, and its story is intertwined with the history of Australian wine. George Wyndham and his descendants were some of the first winemakers to launch Australian wines onto the world stage and to forge a reputation for quality that has endured for more than 175 years.

In 1995 Wyndham Estate began a series of seasonal lunches that have grown to become one of the most popular events in Australia's gourmet calendar, with many diners returning every year to enjoy the atmosphere of celebration and fine dining in a magnificent winery setting.

Over the years, top Australian and international chefs have been invited to create and cook a menu, using produce that reflects each new season and their own unique style of cooking. Legends of the food world, such as Cheong Liew, Tony Bilson, Greg Doyle, Damien Pignolet, Stefano Manfredi and Belgium's Frank Fol as well as some of the newer stars, such as Luke Mangan, Mathew Moran, Darren Simpson, and Guillaume Brahimi have all created exciting menus for their own Seasons Plate lunch.

You will find their recipes, as well as recipes from other great Seasons Plate guest chefs within the pages of this book. There are also profiles of some of the chefs, who share their memories and food philosophies. The Seasons Plate Cookbook forms a fascinating chronicle of this greatly loved event as well as the range and style of food that has been enjoyed over the years.

In the pages that follow, there is an array of dishes to tantalise and tempt you. Some are simple, some are more challenging – all reflect the breadth of talent of this extraordinary group of chefs and will inspire and delight the enthusiastic home cook. Also included are tips to help you make the right wine selection, whatever the dish.

We invite you to share in this unique celebration of the seasons and to bring a touch of Hunter Valley magic into your own kitchen.

Contents

v	INTRODUCTION
2	WYNDHAM ESTATE: A TALE OF SUCCESS
10	WYNDHAM ESTATE WINES
13	THE PERFECT MATCH
16	SPRING
44	SUMMER
74	AUTUMN
104	WINTER
134	CONVERSIONS & COOKING NOTES
135	CHEF DIRECTORY
136	INDEX
138	ACKNOWLEDGEMENTS

*Hunter Valley, 1
Church of England, 0
If George Wyndham's father had had his way, the Hunter Valley — and the Australian wine industry — would never have laid eyes on the man whose influence and name are so closely linked to the region's early success.*

Wyndham Estate: A Tale of Success

Michael Harden

In the early 1800s, William Wyndham, a prosperous estate owner in the English county of Wiltshire, decided that his family needed a representative in the Anglican priesthood and that his third, Cambridge-educated son George would be it. Unfortunately for the Church of England, and luckily for the Hunter Valley, George Wyndham had absolutely no intention of either listening to his father or joining the priesthood and instead set off on a series of adventures, first in Canada and then in Europe.

A couple of important things happened to George on his travels. Firstly, while journeying through France and Italy, George developed a fascination with grape growing and a passion for wine. He determined then and there that, one day, he too would make his own wine. Secondly, amongst his fellow travellers George met a young Belgian woman, Margaret Jay, who was to become his wife. In another demonstration of his determined nature, George followed Margaret to Brussels and married her!

top left: Pioneer vigneron and founder of Wyndham Estate, George Wyndham, 1801–1870.

top right: Dalwood House, located at Wyndham Estate, built by George Wyndham in 1829.

left: Workers at the Dalwood Vineyard in the 1800s.

right: The original basket press which is still used at the winery today.

lower left: The 'new' wine press-room at Dalwood in the late 1800s.

lower right: The cooperage and entrance to the vineyard in the 1870s.

The young couple returned to England for a brief trip so that introductions could be made to the Wyndham family clan. George stayed just long enough to collect a sizeable portion of his inheritance and a flock of his father's prized 'Southdown' sheep. He boarded the SS *George Horn* at the London docks on August 17, 1827, ready to take his new wife, money, sheep, winemaking knowledge and his chances into an unknown future at the other end of the world.

A Spot of Luck

Sometimes you just have to be in the right place at the right time. George and Margaret Wyndham staggered off the SS *George Horn* in Sydney on December 26, 1827, four months after departing England. Their journey had included many of the usual hardships – cramped confines, stormy seas and sparse rations.

Not a man who liked to waste time, George immediately set about looking for land that would suit his plans. He read about a farm of 2,000 acres that was for sale in the recently settled Hunter Valley. Upon learning that the property showed great promise for mixed-use farming, George bought it. He and Margaret and the flock of sheep then set off on the 90-mile bush trek to their new home. Once there, he renamed the property 'Dalwood' after an area of his father's landholdings in England and set about getting the farm in order, not yet realising that he had purchased one of the best grape-growing sites in the country.

In Go the Grapes

George and Margaret's farm would eventually include crops of maize, wheat, hemp, mustard, castor oil, tobacco, millet and cape barley but, reflecting George's true passion and interest, it was the grape vines that took most of his attention in the first year. By the end of 1828 he had planted more than 600 Shiraz vines, Australia's first recorded commercial planting of what has become a calling card for Australian wine overseas. As it happened, the soil and the climate of the Hunter Valley provided ideal growing conditions for Shiraz and there are still vines growing on the site today, making the farm that George built the oldest continuously operating winery in the country.

When they first arrived at the property they were confronted (to the civilised Margaret's horror) with a rudimentary slab hut that was little use in keeping out the hordes of insects and snakes that swarmed about the riverside property. It is not surprising, then, that construction of a more suitable dwelling, Dalwood House, began almost immediately. It showed good foresight to build a house that was, for its time, quite large, because George's family was growing as fast as his grapevines and by 1845 he and Margaret had managed to produce thirteen children.

More, More, More

By 1831 George's grapevines produced their first vintage (even though this early attempt 'promised to make good vinegar') and he had bought another property near Merriwa. Over the next couple of decades George added three more properties to his collection, including a 100,000 acre patch near Inverell where he planted more grapevines. Later vintages of his wine improved markedly and he opened a cellar outlet in Macquarie Street, Sydney, to sell them. George also introduced the first Hereford cattle into mainland Australia, established a thoroughbred racing stud at his Inverell property and instigated the idea of the wine auction into the rapidly expanding local industry.

Of course, even with George's obvious energy, none of his achievements would have been possible without help. In Australia at this time, much of that help was supplied by convicts. George had not realised when he moved to the colonies that he was entitled to one convict for every 100 acres he owned as long as he kept his unpaid labourers fed and housed. It is rumoured that convicts may even have been the reason for Wyndham Estate's unique bin numbering system that is still in use today. The story goes that George needed to devise a system so that his largely illiterate convict workers would be able to identify which wines were stored in different sections of the cellars. The numbering system – Bin 222 for a Chardonnay or Bin 555 for a Shiraz – remains an important part of Wyndham Estate's profile.

By the 1860s George's total vineyard holdings were producing 11,000 gallons of wine per annum. The wines were popular throughout Australia and were being exported in increasing quantities to England and India. At Dalwood, the area under vines had increased to 65 acres of Cabernet, Shiraz and White Hermitage and awards for the wines were piling up. There were silver and bronze medals from the Paris International Exhibition of 1867 and awards in wine shows from Bordeaux to Bombay. George had truly made something of his passion and aptitude for wine.

Baton Changes

George Wyndham died on December 24, 1870 – just three months after the death of his wife Margaret. His many properties were divided amongst his eleven sons and two daughters, with Dalwood going to his son John who had been helping to oversee the Hunter Valley property since the 1850s. John continued to make award-winning wine and ran the property until his death in 1887. Just a few years after John died, Dalwood was awarded the Gold Medal for best Australian wine at Bordeaux.

Over the next few decades, economic recession and financial hardship forced all the properties George had accumulated out of the hands of the Wyndham family. Dalwood continued to operate as a winery under a number of different owners and in 1970 – the 100th anniversary of George Wyndham's death – it was renamed Wyndham Estate in his honour. It was a fitting tribute to George's pioneering work and acknowledgment of his influence on both the direction and perception of the Australian wine industry.

And Now...

Wyndham Estate may have passed out of the Wyndham family's hands but following George Wyndham's early example it is still winning awards and turning heads worldwide. The winery's philosophy of producing wines with generous, full-bodied fruit flavours that accurately represent varietal characteristics is paying off in the form of an ever-growing array of medals from across the world. Since 1996 Wyndham Estate wines have won over 800 Show Awards and are now exported to nearly 50 countries.

The Wyndham Estate philosophy is perhaps best expressed in the 'Bin' Range, where classic varietal characteristics are encouraged and leave you in no doubt about the kind of varietal you are drinking. The Wyndham Estate Bin 222 Chardonnay has genuine Chardonnay varietal characteristics. Likewise, the Bin 444 Cabernet Sauvignon is a straightforward classic of the breed and with the Bin 555 Shiraz you will be sure that you are drinking a Shiraz.

The Wyndham Estate Show Reserve range – a Chardonnay, a Cabernet Merlot and Hunter Valley Semillon and Shiraz – is produced on a smaller scale and represents the pinnacle of winemaking under the Wyndham Estate banner. This is a range that not only receives local and international acclaim but also reflects and pays tribute to the winery's history, in both the style and techniques of winemaking.

And it is not just the wine that is turning heads these days. A constant series of food and entertainment events at the old Dalwood Estate allows a whole new generation of tourists and foodies to appreciate George Wyndham's fortuitous choice of land right on the Hunter River. A 400-seat restaurant and function facility, historic cellar door, beautiful location and stream of international performers at Wyndham Estate's yearly 'Signature Concert' – a rollcall that includes luminaries such as Ray Charles, Shirley Bassey and Sir Cliff Richard – all ensure that Wyndham Estate is a fixture on the maps and minds of the thousands of visitors who flock to the area every year. In addition to the Signature Concerts, Wyndham Estate also hosts annual opera events in a spectacular amphitheatre amongst the vines and, of course, the now iconic Seasons Plate lunches.

A Plate For All Seasons

Four times a year, as one season moves to the next, Wyndham Estate hosts a Seasons Plate lunch at its historic Hunter Valley winery in New South Wales, where up to 400 guests enjoy a specially designed lunch, served on a specially designed plate.

Since the first lunch in 1995, these extremely popular events have attracted sell-out crowds and high calibre chefs. The crowds come to experience the beautiful and historic backdrop of Wyndham Estate winery, exquisitely designed seasonal menus, specially selected Wyndham Estate wines and live musical entertainment.

The chefs who have participated in the Seasons Plate celebrations include a veritable Who's Who of chefs in Australia and a smattering of illustrious chefs from overseas. Much-awarded and revered foodie names such as Cheong Liew, Guillaume Brahimi, Stefano Manfredi, Tony Bilson, Greg Doyle, Damien Pignolet, Serge Dansereau, Luke Mangan and Matthew Moran have all participated in the event over the years; and their presence shows how respected the lunches have become in food circles. It is little wonder that they often sell out within hours.

And yet Seasons Plate lunches could simply be another high-profile, high-quality food and wine affair if not for the unique aspect that gives the event its name. Every Seasons Plate lunch features a specially designed plate which guests can take home as a souvenir. The plates are designed in a block of four, with each of the four designs mirroring the colour or mood of spring, summer, autumn and winter for that year. They are signed by the visiting chef and individually numbered.

The combination of excellent food, wine, music and company might be an age-old formula for fun times, but rarely do all the elements come together simultaneously in a setting as charming as this. The Seasons Plate lunches are happily and truly a unique experience.

Wyndham Estate wines

Bin III Verdelho
An attractive wine with rich fruit flavours, Bin III Verdelho is a classic unwooded style, medium bodied with stunning youthful flavours of lime and melon providing good length on the palate, finishing crisp and dry.

Bin 222 Chardonnay
Offering distinctive varietal fruit flavours with excellent structure and length. Fresh melon and peach fruit aromas with subtle yeast and oak complexity lead to a full, soft palate and a creamy, rich texture as a result of partial oak maturation.

Bin 333 Pinot Noir
An elegant medium bodied red wine with a bouquet of strawberries and cherries, complexed by subtle oak. The palate is full of delicate fruit flavours balanced with soft tannins and a long refined finish.

Bin 444 Cabernet Sauvignon
Deep, rich in colour with full berry fruit and mint flavours. A medium-bodied wine to be savoured now with a variety of red meat or pasta dishes, or cellared to allow further development.

Bin 555 Shiraz
A medium bodied traditional Shiraz with distinct, rich plum and pepper characters coupled with subtle vanillin American oak. Typically rich, but soft structure displaying fine integrated tannins and great length.

Bin 777 Semillon
Bin 777 Semillon displays intense varietal fruit flavours redolent of fresh lemon grass, lime and citrus flavours producing a crisp and refreshing wine, ideal with Asian dishes and al fresco dinning.

Bin 888 Cabernet Merlot
A medium to full-bodied wine displaying ripe blackcurrant, cassis, cherry and spice characters. The elegant and sophisticated palate is enhanced by toasty oak. Blackcurrant and smoky, leafy flavours linger on the finish.

Bin 999 Merlot
This light to medium bodied wine displays flavoursome berry and cherry fruit on the palate, enhanced by soft grape and oak tannins that give balance, length and structure to the wine.

Bin 222 Sparkling Chardonnay
The wine displays fresh lemon and citrus flavours with undertones of creamy yeast. An elegant wine for all occasions.

Bin 555 Sparkling Shiraz
Soft and rounded with full, spicy Shiraz fruit and subtle yeast, Bin 555 Sparkling Shiraz is perfect for any celebration or as an accompaniment to richer meat and game dishes.

Show Reserve Hunter Valley Semillon
This aged release exhibits fresh lemon/lime and straw aromas, leading to a clean stylish palate of citrus and honey. The style rewards cellaring, continuing to develop complexity of flavour for many years to come.

Show Reserve Chardonnay
An exceptional wine, the palate displays ripe, rich and full flavoured peach, melon and fig characters enhanced by well integrated, toasty/nutty oak. Already showing aged characters, the wine will benefit from further cellaring.

Show Reserve Cabernet Merlot
This award winning wine exhibits a complex bouquet of rich cherry and plum fruit with a violet floral background. The blend of varietal characters offers hints of spice and chocolate balanced by fine oak tannins. Excellent cellaring potential with bottle age adding to the wine's complexity.

Show Reserve Hunter Valley Shiraz
The flagship red wine in the range has a complex array of berry, spice and earthy characters for which Hunter Valley is famed. Full Shiraz fruit flavours are supported by soft oak tannins.

The Perfect Match

Peter Bourne

Matching wine with food is often portrayed as a complex and intimidating exercise. It needn't be. Often the simplest combinations are the very best. Slavishly following the tired old axiom 'white wine with fish; red wine with meat' is not the answer, as the colour of a wine may have little to do with its weight, richness and complexity. The key to food and wine pairing is to match the weight of the wine with the richness of the dish, which is often determined by the cooking method and the ancillary ingredients used to create the recipe's sauce or accompaniments.

The structural elements of wine are not dissimilar to those of the raw ingredients used in the kitchen. The depth and intensity of the grape variety's basic fruit flavours is the cornerstone of a good wine, just as the quality of meat, fish and vegetables used in a recipe remains the key to its success.

The structure and balance of a wine is determined by its acid, its tannins and that all important ingredient, alcohol. Acid gives freshness, zest and vitality to a wine, just as a squeeze of lemon lifts the flavour of oysters or deep-fried fish and chips. A good level of acidity enables wine (both red and white) to age gracefully without becoming tired and dull.

Tannin comes from the skins of grapes and gives red wine its grip, bite and astringency to counterbalance the natural sweetness of the grape. Oak barrels provide another source of tannin, giving wooded whites a secondary flavour and adding structure and weight to the finished wine. Quick cooking methods such as barbecuing, grilling or dry roasting add a charry flavour to food, offsetting the natural sweetness of the meat, poultry or fish – similar to the role of tannin in winemaking.

The third element of wine, the alcohol, acts to preserve both the wine and its consumer!

The trick to successful food and wine pairing is to create a balance. Instead of only focussing on the main ingredient of a dish, we also need to take into account the cooking method used and any sauce or other accompaniments. Similarly, as well as thinking about the grape variety, we also need to think about the style of a particular wine.

It is complete nonsense, for instance, to state dogmatically that Chardonnay goes with chicken. For a start, Chardonnays can be quite different in style. It is more important to understand whether the wine is unwooded, or whether it has a rich oak influence, than to focus on the grape variety alone. Similarly, we also need to think about the way the chicken is cooked. Is it to be poached? Roasted with lemon and butter? Coated with spices and char-grilled? Served with a cream and mushroom sauce? Or cooked in red wine, as a classic coq au vin?

Each dish requires a different style of wine with the right structural ingredients to create a harmonious combination, instead of conflict. When in doubt, let the wine underplay the food, not dominate it.

Matches Made in Heaven

Sparkling Chardonnay
is known as Blanc de Blancs in Champagne. The cool fruit flavours of apple and pear are refreshed by the zest of the wine's acidity, making it a perfect aperitif when served solo. It's equally at home with a fresh brie-style cheese or oysters topped with a Japanese-influenced mirin dressing. Sparkling Chardonnay will also add freshness to many desserts: try it with the Sauterne and Olive Oil Cake with Roasted Peaches (page 96).

Sparkling Shiraz
is a uniquely Australian wine. The depth and richness of the red berry fruit flavours are balanced by a touch of residual sweetness and moderated by the time spent on its yeast lees. Sparkling Shiraz is a great match with grilled and barbecue foods, and served with Christmas turkey and ham it makes one of life's great combinations. Try it too as a surprising match with chocolate-based desserts such as the Bitter Chocolate Mousse with Lemon–Coriander Sorbet (page 69).

Verdelho
is at the height of fashion; its generous pineapple and passionfruit flavours make it a wonderful aperitif. Verdelho's natural fruit sweetness lends it to the sweet/sour flavours of many Vietnamese dishes while its straightforward structure also suits simple green leaf salads and seafood dishes. Verdelho would complement beautifully the Salmon Coulibiac with Dill-Yoghurt Dressing (page 28) and its tropical fruit flavours would balance the rich savoury flavours in the Organic Beets and Smoked Swordfish with Landcress, Dill and Horseradish-Crème Fraîche Dressing (page 54). Enjoy it fresh, young and well chilled.

Sauvignon Blanc
is a straightforward variety with flavours of newly mown grass, passionfruit, gooseberry and kiwifruit. Try it with a classic Caesar salad, or with char-grilled chicken breast. Sauvignon Blanc is ideal with lightly spiced foods, especially Thai and Vietnamese where it enjoys the company of fresh coriander. A fruity Sauvignon Blanc would also enhance the complex flavours of Confit of Ocean Trout with Baba Ghanoush and Preserved Lemon Oil (page 114).

Semillon
is a highly underrated grape variety with a split personality. In its youth it is shy and understated. Its light citrus and cut-grass flavours work wonderfully with oysters 'natural' and would perfectly complement the Rotolo of Smoked Salmon, Mascarpone and Salsa Verde (page 82). A young Semillon would also be an interesting match with the curry flavours of the Striped Marlin Loin with Cardamom Sauce, Spicy Potatoes and Peas (page 56). Kept for five or more years Semillon develops rich buttered toast and marmalade flavours while retaining its tight acid structure. This makes it the perfect foil to crayfish served with a lemon butter sauce, while its softness would not be lost on the summery Tomato Salad with Balsamic Syrup, Black Pepper and Green Pea Sorbet (page 50).

Riesling
is perhaps THE most food-friendly variety of wine. Enjoy it young and fresh with Marinated Olives, Semi-dried Tomatoes and Brandade de Morue (page 80) or with light seafood dishes such as Salad of Spanner Crab, Shaved Fennel and Mustard Cress with Citrus Vinaigrette (page 20) or Olive-fried Octopus with Avocado and Pink Grapefruit Salad (page 46). In its maturity, Riesling pairs perfectly with more complex seafood dishes such as Grilled Prawns Three Ways (page 84). Riesling made in a sweet style suits desserts made with summer berries.

Chardonnay
is an amazingly versatile grape, which can be made into a light, fresh, unwooded white wine or a rich, complex and multi-layered blockbuster. Pairing Chardonnay with food needs some thought: oaked Chardonnay is a good match with pork and cream-sauced dishes while the un-oaked versions suit crab dishes, such as the Celeriac Rémoulade with Fresh Crab and Rocket (page 108) and smoked fish recipes such as Salad of Smoked Trout with Chardonnay Dressing (page 48). Try a rich and buttery Chardonnay that has some maturity with a ripe washed-rind cheese such as Hunter Valley Gold.

Pinot Noir

rates on a par with Riesling for food friendliness. It has delicious soft red-berry fruit flavours, while its low levels of structural tannin, compensated by good natural acidity, make it the perfect red for serving with fish – especially with tuna, ocean trout or a salmon dish such as the Confit of Tasmanian Salmon with a Fennel, Red Pepper and Herb Slaw (page 52). Duck and Pinot Noir make perfect partners – try the Crepinette of Duck and Confit Duck with Flageolet Beans and Truffle Oil and Beetroot Purée (page 115) or Slow-Roasted Duck with Steamed Figs, Star Anise and Mustard Fruits (page 89) Sweet baby lamb cutlets, game birds and venison are sublime served with a young Pinot Noir – the delicate flavours of the Seared Venison with Blackberries and Pistachio-Herb Crust (page 34), for instance, would be perfectly matched with a soft Pinot Noir.

Merlot

is as popular with the smart set as Verdelho because its typical sweet plum fruitiness and relatively soft tannin structure make for an easy-drinking red that can be enjoyed in its youth. Try Merlot with casual meals like pizza topped with spicy sausage. A soft fruity Merlot would also be delicious with Roasted Ribeye of Free Range Veal with Garlic, Coppa, Rosemary, Capers, Parsley and Mustard (page 60), or a lamb dish such as Wild Pepper-Crusted Lamb with Pacific Gnocchi and Mint Gremolata (page 121).

Cabernet Sauvignon

is the dominant red grape of the Bordeaux region of France; its bold dark-berry flavours and firm tannin structure make it suitable for long-term cellaring. In its youth Cabernet Sauvignon is best drunk with simply cooked red meats without complex saucing, such as roasted beef fillet or lamb with spinach and roasted vegetables. A full-bodied Cabernet Sauvignon would be perfect with the Prime Beef Tenderloin on Spinach with Vintner's Butter (page 124) or with Roast Suckling 'Ilabo' Lamb with Rosemary and Roast Potatoes (page 31).

Cabernet Sauvignon Merlot

is a typical Bordeaux blend, with the firmer structure of Cabernet Sauvignon softened and rounded out by the sweet juicy-fruited Merlot. In its youth this blend is a willing partner to char-grilled loin lamb chops or generously flavoured pasta dishes such as lasagne or cannelloni. When mature it is the perfect foil for slow-cooked braises and stews or with the rich spiciness of a dish like Seared Hereford Tenderloin Wyndham Estate Style (page 92).

Shiraz

grows well under a variety of climatic conditions, exhibiting pepper berry and spice characters in cool regions and rich blackberry and dark plum flavours in warmer sites. Shiraz adapts equally well to a wide range of dishes. Try a spicy Shiraz with Noisettes of Lamb with Carrot Purée and a Warm Summer Vegetable Salad (page 62). A fuller-bodied Shiraz suits strongly flavoured game and poultry dishes, and red meats cooked almost any way at all. It's a 'true-blue' grape.

Port

is seen as old-fashioned and dull yet it can provide the perfect finale to a structured dinner and makes a warming fireside tipple in winter. Vintage styles benefit from bottle-age and are the classic accompaniment to blue cheese served with a fresh pear. Both vintage and tawny Ports can also make a surprising match with luscious berry-fruit desserts such as Panna Cotta with fresh Raspberries and Grappa Jacopo Poli Pinot (page 71) or Tarte Sablé of Roasted Fruits in Spiced Caramel with Port Wine Granita (page 42).

Liqueur Muscat

is made by fortifying brown muscat grapes with young brandy spirit. The intense grapey fruit flavours are barrel-aged to reveal lush and complex characters that suit the sort of chocolate-based dessert that would scare off most other dessert wines. Try it with the Chocolate and Nougat Tartufo (page 40). Liqueur Muscat also makes a wonderful topping to good quality vanilla ice cream.

Spring in the Hunter Valley; a time of new beginnings; a season of hope and renewal after the chill of winter. In the fields the vines are struck and start to bud. On the table we enjoy the first of the new season's produce.

spring

Burgundy Cheese Puffs

Tony Johansson

250 ml water
90 g butter, cut into pieces
3/4 teaspoon salt
175 g plain flour
4 eggs
150 g gruyère cheese, grated

Preheat the oven to 220°C. Butter 2 baking trays and line with baking parchment.

Put the water, butter and salt into a large heavy-based saucepan. Bring to the boil then remove from the heat. Tip in all the flour at once and beat vigorously with a wooden spoon until the mixture is smooth and comes away cleanly from the side of the pan. Return the pan to a low heat and continue to beat for another minute or so.

Remove from the heat again and add 3 of the eggs, one at a time, beating each one in thoroughly before adding the next. In a separate bowl, whisk the remaining egg. Beat in enough of this remaining egg to make the dough soft and shiny. Stir in the cheese.

Spoon the dough into a piping bag fitted with a 1 cm nozzle. Pipe rounds of dough onto the baking trays, about 5 cm in diameter. Make sure they are well spaced and brush the tops with any remaining egg. Transfer the trays to the oven immediately and bake until golden brown and crisp, about 25–30 minutes.

Makes 24 small puffs

Chardonnay has the body and richness of flavour to balance the cheese in this dish.

I feel food has to be product driven, by obtaining the very best of ingredients and allowing them to speak for themselves. When creating a dish, keep it simple with a limited number of ingredients.

Renowned as Australia's best fish chef, Greg Doyle is the chef and co-owner of the award-winning Pier restaurant in Sydney's Rose Bay. Now in its twelfth year, Pier has been consistently voted Best Seafood restaurant in Sydney's food guides. Greg Doyle's dedicated approach to fish – sourcing, preparing and cooking them – is unequalled, and this rigorous attention to detail extends to all aspects of his restaurant.

Salad of Spanner Crab, Shaved Fennel and Mustard Cress with Citrus Vinaigrette

Salad
3 heads baby fennel
600 g spanner crab meat
200 g mixed baby salad leaves
extra-virgin olive oil
1 punnet mustard cress

Citrus Vinaigrette
20 ml sherry vinegar
20 ml soy sauce
juice of ½ lemon
juice of ½ lime
juice of ½ orange
250 ml extra-virgin olive oil
salt and pepper
50 ml boiling water

Salad
Trim the baby fennel and shave it as finely as you can using a mandolin slicer or very sharp kitchen knife. Prepare salads individually: in a bowl, mix one-sixth of crab meat with some of the shaved fennel and a few salad leaves. Toss with a little olive oil, just so the leaves are very lightly coated.

Citrus Vinaigrette
Place the sherry vinegar, soy sauce and citrus juices in a bowl. Add the extra-virgin olive oil. Add the seasoning and then the boiling water. Stir together but do not whisk.

To Serve
Place a ring mould in the centre of a plate and fill with the mixed salad. Carefully lift off the ring mould, trying to keep some height and structure in the salad. Sprinkle on some mustard cress and drizzle over a couple of tablespoons of citrus vinaigrette. Repeat for the remaining portions and serve the salads straight away.

Serves 6

Prawn Custard with Prawn Bisque

Michael Manners

Prawn Custard
500 g medium-sized raw prawns (reserve shells for bisque)
¼ clove garlic
salt and pepper
2 eggs
250–300 ml pure cream

Prawn Bisque
1 tablespoon olive oil
1 tablespoon butter
prawn shells
1 carrot, diced small
½ onion, diced small
½ celery stick, diced small
50 ml port
25 ml brandy
150 ml white wine
250 ml fish or chicken stock
4 ripe tomatoes, diced small
½ tablespoon chopped fresh tarragon
salt and pepper

Garnish
3 tomatoes
splash of olive oil
salt and pepper
½ teaspoon thyme
watercress sprigs

Prawn Custard
Preheat the oven to 160°C. De-vein the prawns and place them in a blender with the garlic, salt and pepper. Blend to a smooth purée. Blend in the eggs and then enough of the cream to form a light, smooth mixture. Divide between 6 lightly oiled dariole moulds. Place the moulds in a deep baking tray and pour in boiling water to about half the depth of the tray. Cook for 10–15 minutes until the custards are just set. Check from time to time to ensure that the water doesn't boil.

Prawn Bisque
Heat the olive oil and butter in a heavy-based pan then add the prawn shells and sauté until they turn pink. Add the diced vegetables and fry for a few more minutes. Turn up the heat and add the port and brandy. Simmer until reduced by three-quarters. Add the white wine and continue to simmer until reduced by a further three-quarters. Add the stock, diced tomatoes, tarragon and salt and pepper. Lower the heat and simmer gently for 25–30 minutes. Remove from the heat and allow to cool slightly. Pour the stock through a fine sieve. Press with the back of a spoon to extract the maximum liquid. Taste and adjust seasonings if necessary. Reserve until ready to serve.

Garnish
Place the tomatoes on a baking tray, drizzle with oil and season with salt, pepper and thyme. Roast at 160°C until they start to brown, but still maintain their shape. Remove from the oven and cut into rough dice.

To Serve
Carefully unmould the prawn custards and place each one in the centre of a shallow dish. Surround each custard with some bisque and garnish with the oven-roasted tomatoes and a few sprigs of watercress.

Serves 6

Roasted Eggplant, Bocconcini and Peperonata

Stefano Manfredi

Peperonata is a classic Italian dish of sweet red peppers braised with tomatoes and onions and flavoured with garlic and fresh herbs. In this lovely spring entrée, I serve it layered with slices of eggplant and bocconcini (baby mozzarella balls) to form a sort of double-decker sandwich!

3 medium eggplant
   (6–8 cm diameter)
salt
olive oil
6 bocconcini, thinly sliced

Peperonata
6 tablespoon extra-virgin olive oil
2 large red capsicums, cut into large pieces
2 medium onions, cut into chunks
2 cloves garlic, minced
4 roma tomatoes, roughly chopped
a handful of fresh basil leaves
salt and pepper

Preheat the oven to 220°C. Cut the eggplant into slices 1 cm thick and sprinkle on both sides with a little salt. Layer the eggplant slices in a colander and leave in the sink for 10 minutes. Rinse off the salt and pat the slices dry. Brush each slice with a little olive oil, arrange on a baking tray and roast in the oven for 5–10 minutes, or until golden brown. Remove from the oven and leave to cool.

Peperonata
Heat the olive oil in a large heavy-based saucepan. Add the red peppers, onion and garlic. Turn up the heat and fry for a few minutes, stirring with a wooden spoon, until the peppers, onion and garlic start to wilt. Add the tomatoes, lower the heat and simmer for 20 minutes. Stir from time to time. Add the basil, salt and pepper and leave to cool.

To Serve
Place a slice of eggplant on each plate and spoon over a little peperonata. Top with a slice of bocconcini. Repeat the layering with eggplant, peperonata and bocconcini, finishing with a top layer of eggplant.

Serves 6

This is an entrée with interesting and subtle flavours. A crisp, minerally Riesling or Pinot Gris will serve as a delicate accompaniment and leave a clean finish on the palate.

Warm Honey-Glazed Quail on a Potato Galette with Snowpea Salad

Tony Johansson

It is best to parboil the potatoes the day before so they can chill in the refrigerator overnight. They should be quite firm and definitely not overcooked. This dish may also be served as a main course, in which case allow 2 quails per person.

Honey-glazed Quail
6 x 200 g jumbo quail
olive oil
salt and pepper
25 ml port
25 g butter
100 ml good quality beef stock
2 tablespoons Leatherwood honey
 (or your favourite)
100 g pine nuts, lightly toasted

Potato Galette
500 g peeled potatoes, parboiled
 and refrigerated overnight
1 egg, beaten
pinch of salt and pepper
3 tablespoons olive oil

Snowpea Salad
100 ml olive oil
50 ml balsamic vinegar
1 teaspoon Dijon mustard
good squeeze of lemon juice
1 clove garlic, crushed
salt and pepper to taste
300 g snowpea leaves
 (or any other mix of
 interesting salad leaves)

Honey-glazed Quail
Trim the quail of their necks and wing tips. Use a sharp knife or scissors and cut each quail along the breast-plate, then use your hand to flatten them out.

Preheat the oven to 150°C. In a heavy-based frying pan, heat the olive oil and fry the quail, skin side down until lightly brown. Season with salt and pepper, turn and cook the other side (around 4 minutes per side). Keep warm until ready to serve.

When all quails are cooked, deglaze the pan with the port. Add the butter and allow to simmer until the butter has melted. Add the stock, and simmer until reduced by one-third. Stir in the honey and keep until ready to serve.

Potato Galettes
Grate the potatoes into a large bowl and add the beaten egg, salt and pepper and 1 tablespoon of the olive oil. Mix lightly. Heat the remaining olive oil in a heavy-based frying pan. Drop in spoonfuls of potato mixture and press gently to form pancakes around 10–15 cm in diameter. Fry on both sides until golden brown. Keep warm in the oven while you cook the remaining pancakes. Alternatively, make one large galette and cut into wedges to serve.

Snowpea Salad
Combine the olive oil, vinegar, mustard, lemon juice, garlic and seasonings to make the dressing. Dress the snowpea leaves lightly, just before serving.

To Serve
Place a potato galette in the centre of each plate and top with a small mound of salad. Dip each quail into the hot honey-glaze, allowing the excess to drain away. Lay the quail on the salad and drizzle over a little extra honey-glaze. Sprinkle with pine nuts and serve.

Serves 6 as an entrée

Michael Manners

Cooking for large numbers of people can be challenging, to say the least! The Seasons Plate lunch at Wyndham Estate was a pleasure from start to finish, thanks to the wonderful hospitality and enthusiasm of everyone involved, the gorgeous setting and the relaxed, celebratory atmosphere.

Michael Manners is one of Australia's most successful country chefs, with a passion for sourcing and promoting the very best regional produce. He started his career studying hotel management in Switzerland and has spent an impressive four decades in the industry. Michael is much admired for his skill and artistry with simple, top-quality ingredients. His menus feature his own unique rustic versions of modern Australian cuisine. Michael's award-winning restaurant, Selkirks, is located in Orange in western New South Wales.

Roasted Chicken on Spring Vegetable Ragoût

With its fresh colourful vegetables and new season's herbs, this dish represents Spring, in all its glory. Use a selection of whatever vegetables look best – those suggested below serve as guidelines. If possible, prepare the chickens a day ahead of time to allow the herbs to infuse.

6 x No 4 or 6 baby chickens, corn-fed preferably
100 ml olive oil
salt and pepper
600 ml chicken stock
squeeze of lemon juice

Herb Butter
a few sprigs each of fresh thyme, rosemary and parsley
1 clove garlic, finely chopped
200 g softened butter
salt and pepper
juice of $1/2$ lemon

Ragoût of Spring Vegetables
12 small shallots
12 baby carrots
12 baby button mushrooms
12 baby chat potatoes, cut in half
12 sugar snap peas or green beans
12 small asparagus spears
a few handfuls of baby spinach
60 ml olive oil
1 tablespoon butter
200 ml chicken stock
1 tablespoon finely chopped chives
1 tablespoon finely chopped chervil
1 tablespoon finely chopped parsley

Herb Butter
To make the herb butter, finely chop the herbs. Add to the remaining ingredients and mix thoroughly.

Prepare the chickens by stuffing each one under the skin with the herb butter. Rub all over with half the olive oil and season with salt and pepper. Leave overnight for the flavours to infuse.

When ready to cook, preheat the oven to 180°C. Heat the remaining olive oil in a heavy-based frying pan and sear the birds until they are coloured all over. Place a wire rack in a deep baking dish and arrange the chickens on top. Roast for about 40 minutes, or until the chickens are cooked. Remove from the oven and leave the chickens in a warm place to rest. Deglaze the baking dish with the chicken stock to make a gravy, then strain and reserve until ready to serve.

Ragoût of Spring Vegetables
Wash and trim the vegetables of your choice. Heat the olive oil and butter in a heavy-based frying pan and sauté the shallots and carrots until they start to soften. Add the mushrooms and cook for a further few minutes. Add the stock and simmer until the vegetables are just tender. This becomes the base for the vegetable ragoût.

Meanwhile, boil the chat potatoes, sugar snaps and asparagus until just tender. Strain and add to the shallots and carrots. Simmer gently, and just before you are ready to serve, add the spinach and chopped herbs.

To Serve
Reheat the chicken gravy, skimming off any excess fat that rises to the surface. Simmer until reduced by half. Add a squeeze of lemon then taste and adjust seasonings if necessary.

Ladle a generous amount of spring vegetable ragoût onto each plate and arrange a spatchcock on top. Serve with the gravy on the side.

Serves 6

Choose a full-bodied, rich Chardonnay to match the flavour of the chicken.

Salmon Coulibiac with Dill-Yoghurt Dressing

Tony Johansson

These Russian fish pies can be made as individual parcels or one large pie, using a whole boned side of salmon. Coulibiac is delicious served hot or cold. It keeps well in the fridge for up to three days.

300 g millet, soaked
   overnight in cold water
4 hard-boiled eggs, roughly chopped
100 g sun-dried tomatoes, chopped
½ cup finely chopped parsley
salt and pepper
6 sheets ready-rolled puff pastry
6 x 200 g pieces of salmon fillet,
   pin bones removed
1 beaten egg

Dill-Yoghurt Dressing
200 g natural yoghurt
juice of ½ lemon
½ cup finely chopped fresh dill
salt and pepper

Drain the millet well and squeeze out any excess water. Place in a large bowl with the hard-boiled eggs, sundried tomatoes and parsley and mix well. Season with salt and pepper.

Preheat the oven to 225°C. Lay each sheet of pastry out on a lightly floured work surface. Place 1 salmon fillet on each piece of pastry, approximately 2 cm from one edge. Spoon a generous mound of millet along the top of the salmon, carefully building it up to a height of about 2 cm. Brush the edges of the pastry with a little beaten egg and fold the large side of pastry up and over the salmon, sealing along the 3 sides. Trim away excess pastry, and crimp the edges with a fork. Brush each pastry parcel with more beaten egg and prick the top twice with the point of a sharp knife. Carefully place the salmon parcels on a greased baking tray and bake for 20–25 minutes, until golden brown. (The cooking time will depend on your oven.)

Dill-Yoghurt Dressing
Tip the yoghurt into a mixing bowl and stir in the lemon juice, chopped dill, salt and pepper. Stir well, taste and adjust flavourings to taste.

To Serve
Cut each coulibiac in half on an angle and place in the centre of each plate. Spoon on a generous amount of dressing and garnish with a sprig of dill. Serve with steamed green beans or a mixed leaf salad.

Serves 6

Sauvignon Blanc or Semillon-Sauvignon Blanc will work well with this dish. Their soft, fruity flavours are fresh enough to balance the richness of the salmon and yoghurt, but will not dominate.

Mignonettes of Lamb with Sweet Roasted Garlic, Creamed Potatoes and Rosemary Jus

Greg Doyle

6 x 7 point lamb racks
100 g chopped parsley
10 g chopped thyme
10 g herbes de provence
25 g garlic, finely chopped
salt and pepper

Creamed Potatoes
2 kg desirée potatoes
salt
250 g unsalted butter
125 ml pure cream
60 ml extra-virgin olive oil
salt and white pepper

Sweet Roasted Garlic
2 heads of garlic
30 ml olive oil
1 tablespoon caster sugar

Rosemary Jus
250 ml lamb jus or reduced stock
a few sprigs of rosemary

Trim the lamb of fat and sinews and carefully slice it away from the bones, keeping it in one piece. In a shallow dish mix together the herbs, garlic, salt and pepper. Roll each piece of lamb in the herb mixture so that they are evenly coated. Cover the lamb pieces with cling film and refrigerate for a minimum of 4 hours or, preferably, overnight.

Creamed Potatoes
Peel the potatoes and put them in a saucepan with plenty of cold water. Bring to the boil and salt the water generously. Cook until very tender, then drain well. Add the butter, cream and extra-virgin olive oil to the pan and whisk to a smooth purée. Keep warm until ready to serve.

Sweet Roasted Garlic
Preheat a baking dish in a 200°C oven. Separate the garlic into cloves, leaving on the skins. Scatter the garlic cloves into the hot baking dish and drizzle over the olive oil. Roast for 10–15 minutes, or until the garlic is soft and cooked. Sprinkle over the sugar and return to the oven for a further 5 minutes. Once the sugar has caramelised, remove from the oven.

Meanwhile, cook the lamb: sear the lamb pieces in a heavy-based ovenproof tray then roast in the hot oven for 5–7 minutes for medium-rare. Remove from the oven and leave to rest in a warm place for 5–10 minutes.

To Serve
Reheat the lamb jus with the rosemary and allow to simmer for a few moments. Spoon some creamed potatoes in the centre of each plate. Slice the lamb mignonettes into 3 pieces and arrange them around the potato. Scatter over the caramelised garlic cloves, drizzle with rosemary jus and serve.

Serves 6

Roast Suckling 'Ilabo' Lamb with Rosemary and Roast Potatoes

Stefano Manfredi

Like all good Italian cooking, the secret to this dish is the quality of the ingredients. Try to find a butcher who can supply you with suckling (milk-fed) lamb. In the restaurant we use the outstanding Ilabo lamb from south-western New South Wales. Suckling lamb is mild-flavoured and exquisitely tender. It is at its best when partnered with the classics: rosemary and roast potatoes. Use waxy potatoes like desirée or pinkeye (the latter take a little longer to cook).

2 x suckling lamb legs, trimmed of excess flaps
120 ml olive oil
salt and pepper
1 big bunch fresh rosemary
2 kg desirée potatoes, peeled and cut into bite-sized chunks

Preheat the oven to 220°C. Rub the lamb legs all over with the olive oil and season well with salt and pepper. Scatter some sprigs of rosemary in the bottom of a large baking dish and arrange the lamb on top. Roast for 20–25 minutes then remove from the oven and leave in a warm place to rest for a further 20 minutes.

At the same time, roast the potatoes. Place them in a baking tray and drizzle generously with olive oil. Scatter on some small sprigs of rosemary and season with salt and pepper. Toss well so that all the potatoes are coated in oil. Roast in the oven with the lamb for 20–25 minutes, tossing them around from time to time, so they brown evenly.

Slice the lamb and serve it drizzled with some of the pan juices and the roast potatoes. Serve with steamed new season vegetables.

Serves 6

Choose a good Cabernet Sauvignon or Merlot for fruit and softness.

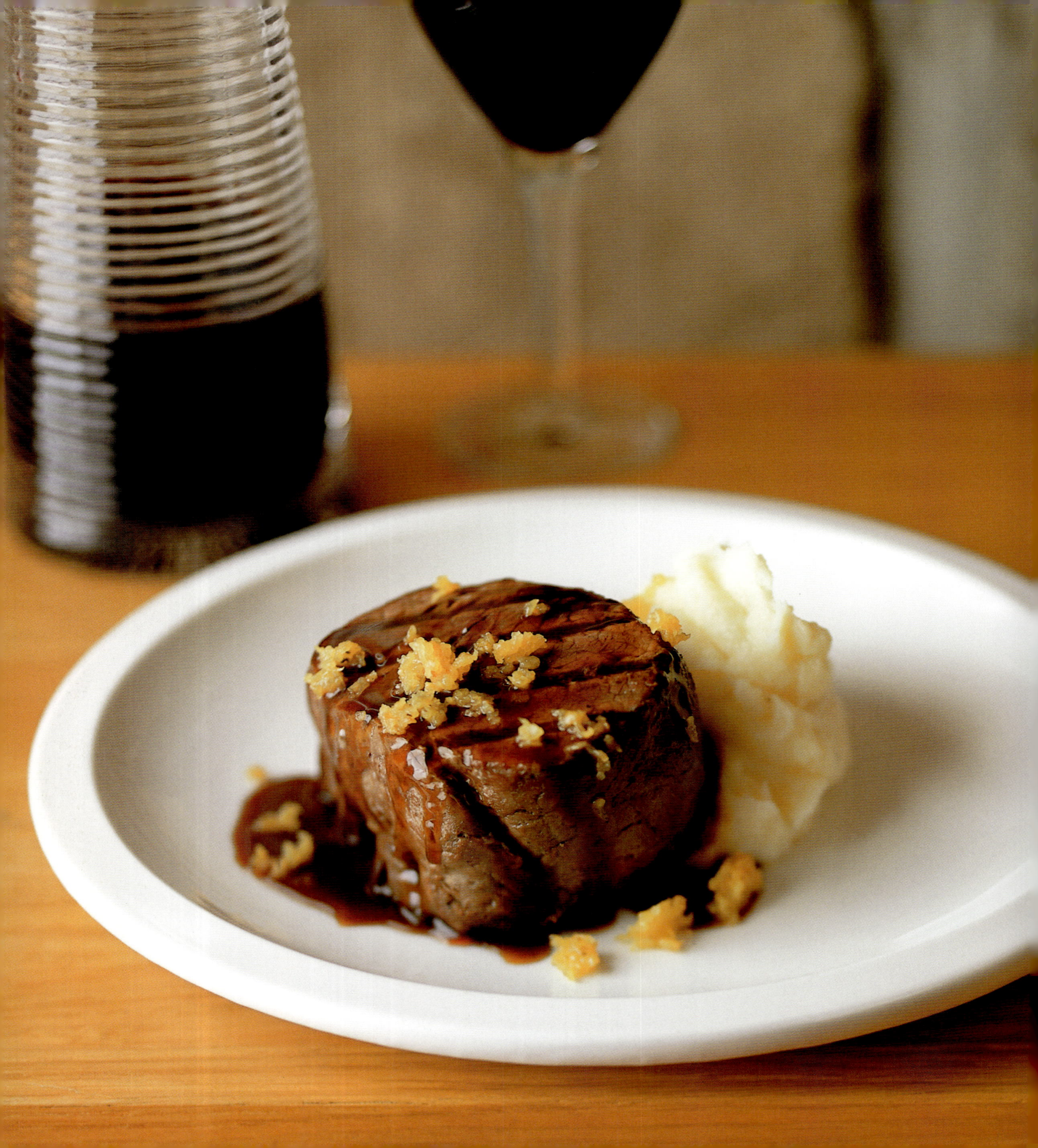

Roast Beef Tenderloin with Shallot Confit, Paris Mash and Merlot Sauce

6 x 200 g pieces of beef tenderloin
olive oil
salt and pepper

Shallot Confit
6 shallots, finely chopped
100 g butter
salt and pepper

Paris Mash
600 g desirée potatoes, skins on
100 g butter
300 ml warm milk
salt and pepper

Merlot Sauce
1 carrot, finely diced
1 medium onion, finely chopped
1 small bunch thyme
1 teaspoon freshly ground white pepper
600 ml merlot

Shallot Confit
Melt the butter in a heavy-based frying pan. Add the shallots and cook over a very gentle heat until golden brown, about 15–20 minutes. Season with salt and pepper to taste.

Paris Mash
Put the potatoes in a large pan of cold, salted water. Bring to the boil and cook until they are tender. Drain well and peel the potatoes when they are cool enough to handle. Use a moulis, potato ricer or hand masher to purée the potatoes. Return the potatoes to the saucepan and leave to steam dry. Just before serving add the butter and warm milk and mix well. Taste and adjust seasoning if necessary.

Roast Beef Tenderloin
Preheat the oven to 220°C. Brush the pieces of beef with a little olive oil and season with salt and pepper. Seal the beef in a hot frying pan so it is evenly coloured all over. Transfer the beef to an ovenproof tray and roast for 5 minutes for medium-rare, or until done to your liking. Remove from the oven and leave in a warm place to rest for 10 minutes.

Merlot Sauce
Put the diced carrots, onion, thyme and pepper in the same frying pan used to seal the beef. Stir well then add the merlot and bring to a boil. Lower the heat and simmer until reduced by half. Strain the sauce through a fine sieve.

To Serve
Place a spoonful of mash in the centre of each plate. Arrange a piece of beef on the potato and top with a spoonful of shallot confit. Drizzle the plate with the merlot sauce and serve straight away.

Serves 6

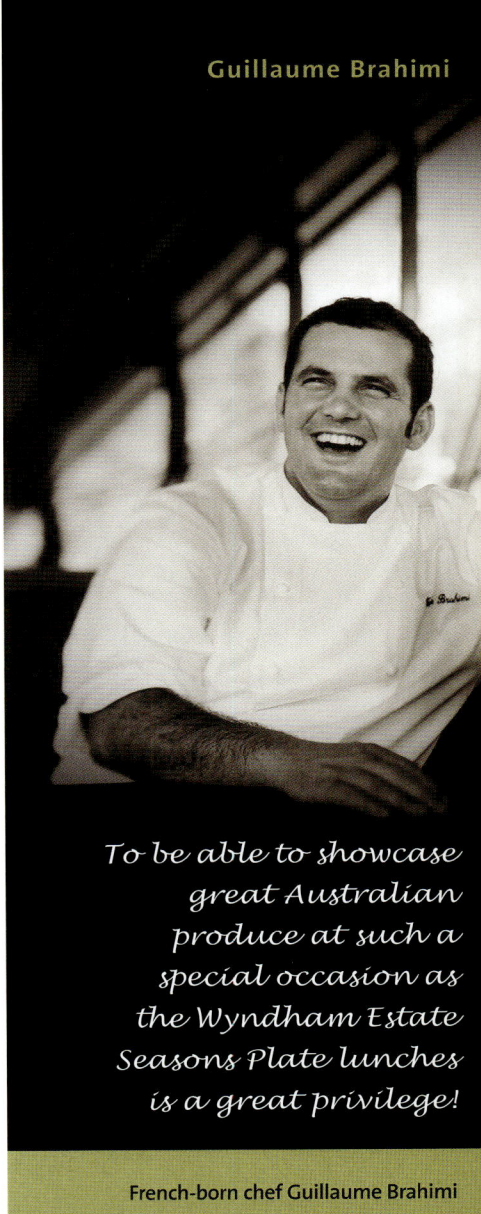

Guillaume Brahimi

To be able to showcase great Australian produce at such a special occasion as the Wyndham Estate Seasons Plate lunches is a great privilege!

French-born chef Guillaume Brahimi began his illustrious cooking career in Paris in the Michelin three-star restaurants, La Tour d'Argent and Jamin. Since moving to Sydney, the accolades have continued. He is currently earning rave reviews for his superbly crafted modern French-influenced food at Guillaume at Bennelong, next to the Sydney Opera House.

Seared Venison with Blackberries and Pistachio-Herb Crust

Ian Burrows

This is an intensely flavoured and rich dish, and is ideally served with some simply steamed spinach and fondant potatoes.

6 x 150 g venison loin medallions
sea salt and freshly ground pepper
20 ml clarified butter
small sprigs of marjoram for garnish

Pistachio-Herb Crust
50 g brioche crumbs or breadcrumbs
50 g pistachio nuts, peeled and
   finely chopped
¼ cup finely chopped parsley
¼ cup finely chopped marjoram
¼ cup finely chopped thyme
30 g unsalted butter, softened

Blackberry Sauce
50 ml olive oil
1 teaspoon butter
8 large shallots, peeled and diced
2 bay leaves
1 large sprig of thyme
pinch of roughly cracked
   black pepper
250 ml red wine vinegar
250 ml ruby port
750 ml full-bodied red wine
1.75 litres good quality veal stock *
10 ml crème de mûre
   (blackcurrant crème liqueur)
10 ml pistachio oil (available from
   good delicatessens)
36 whole blackberries

Pistachio-Herb Crust
Place all the ingredients in a food processor and blend well.

Blackberry Sauce
Melt the olive oil and butter in a medium saucepan. Add the shallots, herbs and black pepper and sweat gently until shallots are soft, but do not allow them to colour. Add the vinegar and turn the heat up. Boil vigorously until reduced by two-thirds.

Add the port and red wine and continue cooking until reduced to around 200 ml. Add the veal stock and simmer for 25–30 minutes, or until the sauce has reduced by half, to around 1 litre. Strain through a double thickness muslin cloth to obtain a rich, clear sauce and return to a clean saucepan. Just before you are ready to serve, add the crème de mûre, the pistachio oil and whole blackberries. Keep the sauce warm, but do not allow it to boil.

Seared Venison
Preheat the oven to its highest temperature (230°C). Season the meat well with salt and pepper. Heat the clarified butter in a heavy-based ovenproof pan and brown the meat so it is evenly coloured all over. Place in the oven and cook for 2 minutes. Turn the meat and cook for a further 6 minutes. Remove from the oven and sprinkle the pistachio-herb crust over the meat. Leave in a warm place to rest for 5 minutes.

To Serve
Arrange the venison medallions on each plate and serve with steamed spinach and fondant potatoes. Drizzle with a little blackberry sauce, making sure that each plate gets 6 blackberries. Garnish with a few sprigs of fresh marjoram.

Serves 6
* Note: Home-made veal stock is the key to making the sauce for this dish. The natural gelatine gives it substance and body that is impossible to obtain elsewhere. A good quality beef stock will suffice, but the result will not be as good.

Choose a light-bodied Pinot Noir or Grenache to serve with this venison. The spicy, berry flavours will not overwhelm the delicate meat and will complement the blackberry sauce.

Orange Pot au Crème, Orange Sorbet and Orange Salad

Greg Doyle

The quantities below make enough for 12 serves, but it is best to make this amount as the recipe for the custard works better. You can serve the extra custard with dessert for the next few days.

Orange Pot au Crème
750 ml pure cream (45% fat)
250 g caster sugar
8 large egg yolks
50 ml Cointreau

Orange Sorbet
1 kg caster sugar
700 ml water
1 litre fresh orange juice

Orange Sauce
6 oranges
250 g caster sugar
250 ml still mineral water

Orange Salad
3–4 oranges

Orange Pot au Crème
Preheat the oven to 175°C. Lightly grease 12 small ovenproof moulds and place them in a deep baking dish. Put the cream and sugar in a heavy-based saucepan and warm gently until the sugar dissolves. The cream should be warm rather than hot. In a separate bowl, whisk the egg yolks gently until they are pale and creamy, but make sure they do not become foamy. Slowly pour the warm cream onto the egg yolks, stirring continuously. Strain the mixture through a fine sieve and stir in the Cointreau. Pour the mixture into the moulds, filling each one right to the top. Pour hot water into the baking tray, to about halfway up the height of the moulds. Cook for about 30 minutes, or until the custards are just set (they should still be a little wobbly in the centre). Check from time to time to ensure that the water doesn't boil. Remove from the oven and place the moulds on a rack to cool. Refrigerate until ready to serve.

Orange Sorbet
Place the sugar and water in a heavy-based pan and heat gently to dissolve the sugar. Once clear, bring to the boil for 1 minute, then remove from the heat and leave to cool. Strain the orange juice through a fine sieve. Measure 600 ml of the sugar syrup and stir into the orange juice. Pour into an ice cream machine and churn according to the manufacturer's instructions.

Orange Sauce
Use a vegetable peeler or sharp paring knife to peel the skin away from the oranges. Make sure there is no pith attached to the skin. Slice the orange peel into fine julienne strips. Juice the oranges and strain through a sieve into a heavy-based saucepan. Add the sugar and mineral water to the pan and heat gently until the sugar dissolves. Add the julienne of orange peel and bring to the boil. Lower the heat and simmer until it thickens to form a heavy syrup, about 10–15 minutes. Leave to cool.

Orange Salad
Peel the skin and membrane off the oranges. Using a sharp knife, carefully cut down each side of the membrane between each segment. Flip the segments out into a bowl.

To Serve
Place a pot au crème in the centre of each plate. Next to it, arrange a scoop of orange sorbet in a small dish. Place about 5 or 6 orange segments on the plate. Drizzle some of the orange sauce over the oranges with some of the rind. Place a little orange sauce on top of the custard to give it a vibrant colour. Serve straight away.

Serves 12

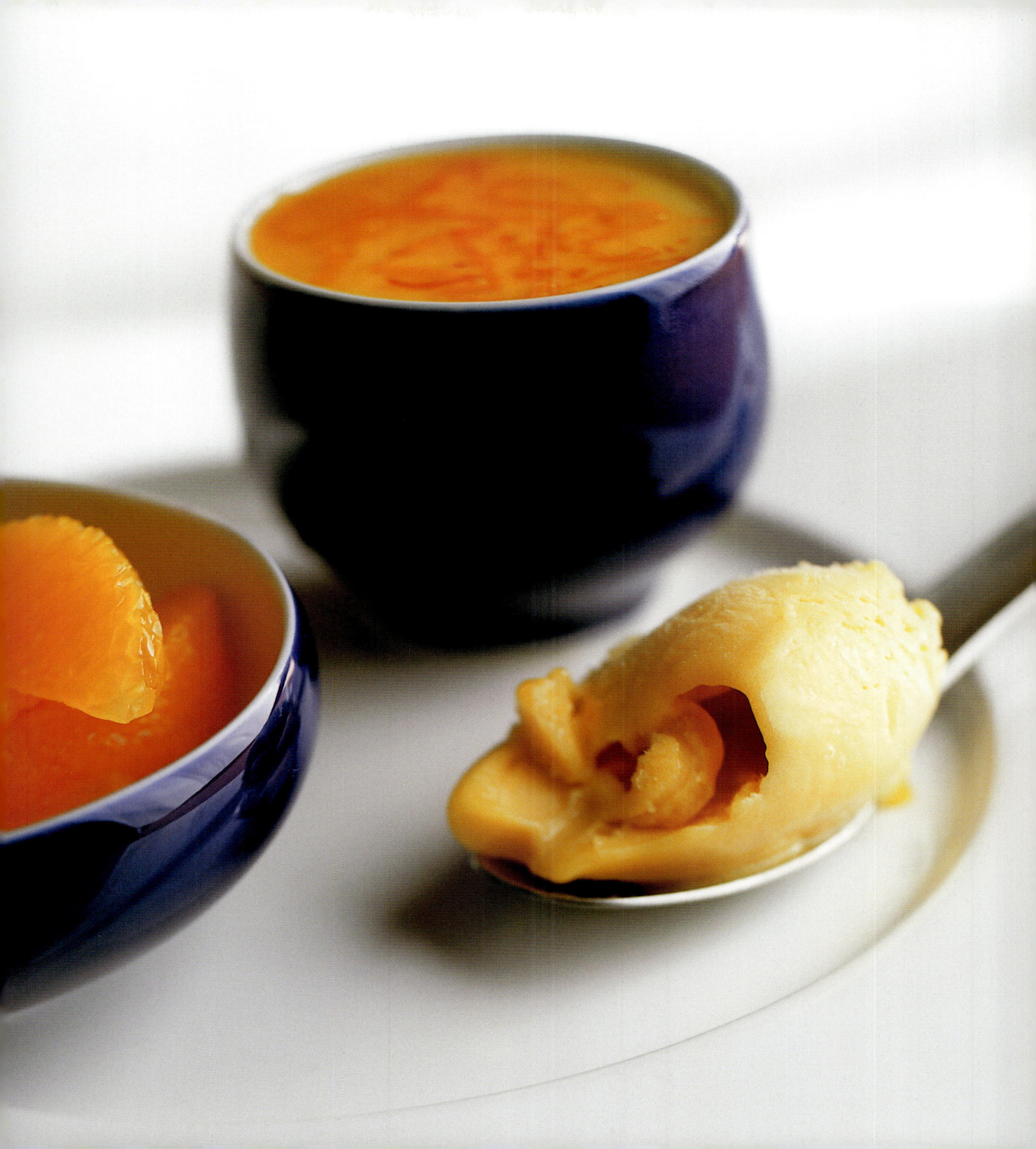

Infused Poached Pears with Vanilla Bean Ice Cream

Guillaume Brahimi

Beurre bosc or William pears are ideal for this elegant and simple dessert. They can be poached well in advance and stored in the refrigerator. Bring to room temperature to serve.

600 g caster sugar
600 ml water
6 pears, peeled,
    but with stems attached
½ lemon
1 star anise
1 cinnamon stick

Vanilla Bean Ice Cream
400 ml milk
7 egg yolks
160 g caster sugar
240 ml cream
1 vanilla bean,
    split and seeds scraped

To poach the pears, put the sugar and water in a large heavy-based pan and heat gently until the sugar has dissolved. Arrange the pears in the pan and add the lemon, star anise and cinnamon stick. Simmer gently until the pears are tender – the time will vary depending on the ripeness of the pears. Remove from the heat and leave to cool in the poaching syrup.

Vanilla Bean Ice Cream
Put the milk in a saucepan and bring to the boil. In a separate bowl, whisk together the egg yolks and sugar until light and creamy, then whisk in the hot milk. Return to a rinsed-out pan and cook over a gentle heat, stirring constantly, until the mixture thickens enough to coat the back of a spoon. Strain through a chinois or fine sieve. Allow to cool a little, then add the cream and vanilla seeds, stirring well. Pour into an ice cream machine and churn according to the manufacturer's instructions.

To Serve
Place the pears in shallow bowls, accompanied by a generous scoop of ice cream. Drizzle with a little poaching syrup and serve straight away.

Serves 6

Bruléed Rhubarb Tart

Michael Manners

The quantities below will make more pastry than you require, but it freezes perfectly well for use in another sweet tart. If there is too much rhubarb, it is delicious for breakfast!

Brulée
500 ml pure cream
peel of 1 lemon
½ stick cinnamon
½ vanilla bean, split and scraped
small piece ginger, grated
4 egg yolks
50 g caster sugar
about 6 extra tablespoons sugar to brulée

Pastry
100 g flaked almonds
400 g plain flour
125 g caster sugar
pinch salt
350 g cold butter, diced
2 eggs

Rhubarb
1 kg rhubarb
3 tablespoons caster sugar
3 tablespoons water

Brulée
To make the brulée, put the cream in a heavy-based saucepan with the lemon peel, cinnamon, vanilla bean and ginger. Bring to a boil then turn off the heat and leave to infuse for 20 minutes.

In a separate bowl, whisk together the egg yolks and sugar. Pour on the infused cream and whisk well. Rinse and dry the saucepan and pour the custard mix back in. Cook over a medium heat until the custard thickens, about 10 minutes. When the custard is ready, remove from the heat and strain through a sieve. Leave it to cool, then refrigerate overnight.

Pastry
Put the almonds into a food processor and pulse to a coarse meal. Add the flour, sugar and salt and pulse to combine. Then add the butter and pulse to a sandy consistency. Add the eggs and pulse quickly until the mixture just comes together. Tip the pastry out of the bowl, wrap it in plastic and refrigerate for at least 20 minutes before rolling it out and lining 6 small deep tart tins. Place tins in the freezer for a further 20 minutes.

Preheat the oven to 200°C. Bake the tarts blind for about 12 minutes then bake for a further 3–5 minutes, or until they turn golden brown and the pastry is cooked through. Remove from the oven and leave to cool on a wire rack.

Rhubarb
Trim and wash the rhubarb. Cut into 2 cm pieces and place in a heavy-based saucepan. Add the sugar and water, toss well and cook, covered, for around 10–15 minutes, or until tender. Drain the rhubarb, reserving the juice. Return the juice to the pan, and simmer until it is reduced to a syrup.

To Serve
Fill the pre-baked pastry shells about three-quarters full with rhubarb, then pour over enough chilled custard to fill the tarts generously. Sprinkle with the extra sugar and brulée with a blow torch. Serve with the rhubarb syrup.

Serves 6

Choose a sweet sparkling white wine – not a traditional choice for dessert, but the inherent fruit sweetness of the wine will harmonise with the fruit tart, while the freshness of the bubbles will keep the end result from being cloying.

Stefano Manfredi

For me, working with chefs in regional Australia has always been a passion and a highlight in my career. Working on the Seasons Plate lunches gave me the opportunity to be involved in a wonderful cultural event and do what I do best - feed people.

Born in Lombardy in Northern Italy, Stefano Manfredi migrated to Australia with his family in 1961. With the success of successive restaurants, The Restaurant, Restaurant Manfredi, bel mondo and la Mensa, Stefano has cemented his role as one of Australia's most influential Italian chefs. Awards have included best NSW restaurant, three Chef's Hats and the Insegna del Ristorante from the Italian government. Stefano is in constant demand as a guest speaker and has written two successful books: *Fresh from Italy: Italian cooking for the Australian kitchen* and *bel mondo: beautiful world*.

Chocolate and Nougat Tartufo

Ice Cream Base
750 ml thickened cream (35% fat)
50 g honey
6 egg yolks
100 g caster sugar

Chocolate Cream
150 g best quality dark chocolate
100 ml thickened cream (35% fat)

The Dry Mix
2 cups shredded coconut
½ cup whole raw peanuts, blanched
½ cup whole raw almonds, cut into small pieces
250 g hard Italian nougat, cut into small dice

Coconut Custard
½ cup of the roasted coconut threads, see above
600 ml pure cream (45% fat)
4 egg yolks
100 g caster sugar

Ice Cream Base
Put the cream in a heavy-based saucepan with the honey and slowly bring to the boil. Meanwhile, in a separate bowl, whisk the egg yolks and sugar until pale and creamy. When the cream is on the point of boiling, pour it onto the egg mixture and whisk well. Return the mixture to the pan and cook on a very low heat, stirring continuously with a wooden spoon. When the mixture is thick enough to coat the back of a spoon remove it from the heat and strain it through a fine sieve into a chilled bowl. When the custard is cold, tip into an ice cream machine and churn to a soft ice cream.

Chocolate Cream
Chop the chocolate into small pieces. Place the cream in a heavy-based saucepan and bring to the boil. Remove from the heat and whisk in the chocolate. Set aside to cool.

The Dry Mix
Roast the dry ingredients separately in a low oven (100–120°C) until they are lightly browned. Set aside and leave to cool.

When the chocolate cream and the roasted ingredients are cool, mix them together, reserving 1 cup of the coconut for later use. Stir until well combined and add to the soft ice cream. Mix well then spoon into 12 small moulds and freeze overnight.

Coconut Custard
Place ½ cup of the reserved roasted coconut in a pan with the cream. Bring to the boil, then remove from the heat and leave for 30 minutes to infuse. Strain through a fine cloth and return the cream to a clean pan. Bring the cream slowly to the boil. Meanwhile, in a separate bowl, whisk the egg yolks and sugar until pale and creamy. When the cream is on the point of boiling, pour it onto the egg mixture and whisk well. Return the mixture to the pan and cook on a very low heat, stirring continuously with a wooden spoon. When the mixture is thick enough to coat the back of a spoon remove it from the heat and strain it through a fine cloth into a chilled bowl. Cover and set aside to cool.

To Serve
Unmould the tartufi and roll each one in the remaining roasted coconut. Serve with the coconut custard.

Makes 12 individual tartufi

The sweet, nutty chocolate flavours of this dessert will stand up well to a luscious, complex yet fruity Liqueur Muscat.

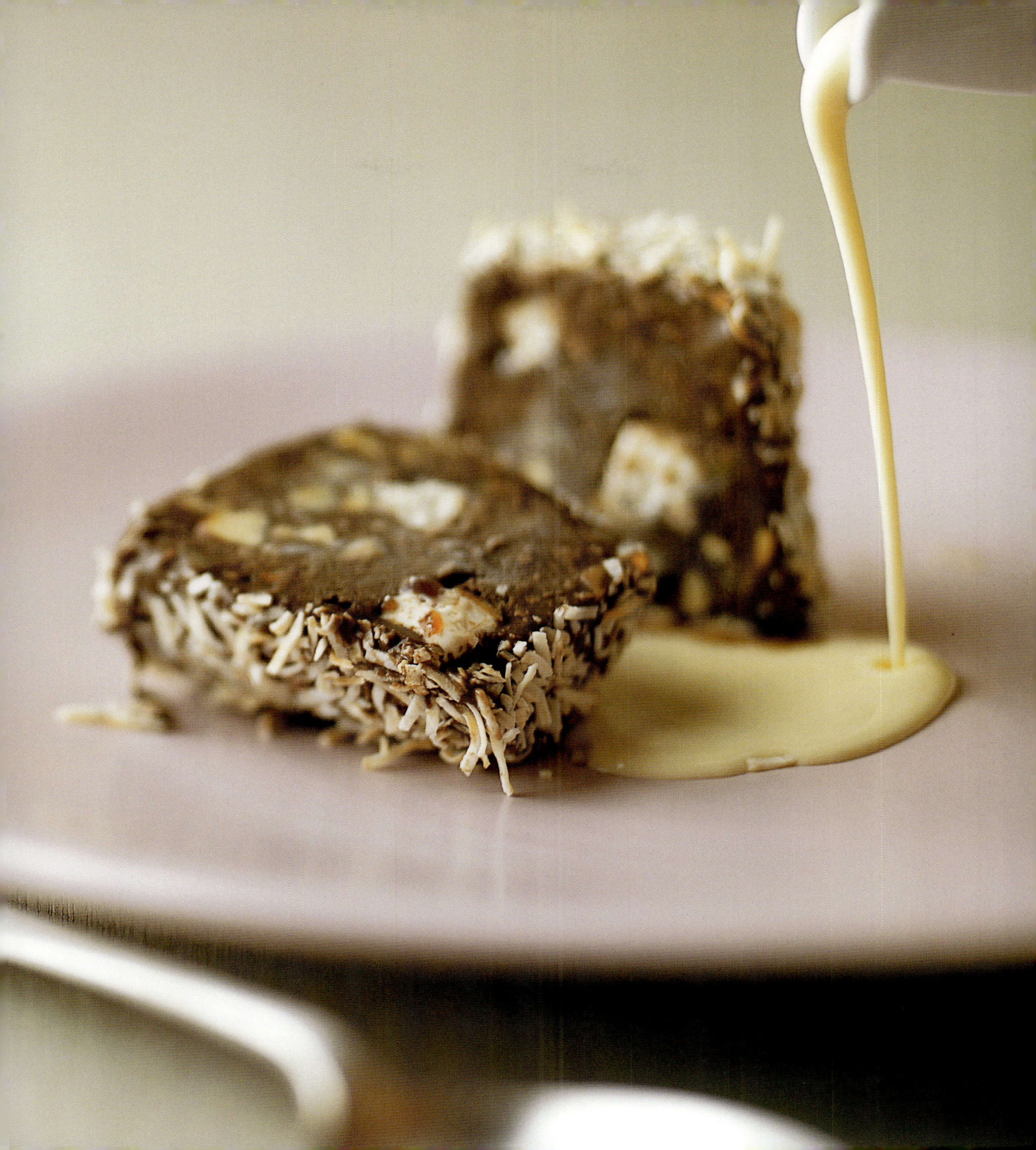

Tarte Sablé of Roasted Fruits in Spiced Caramel with Port Wine Granita

Ian Burrows

All types of fruit work well in these tarts, and this will vary according to season. Try to select a range that will give a good balance of texture, sweetness and acidity. Most importantly, choose top quality, perfectly ripe fruit.

Sablé Pastry (Shortbread)
400 g unsalted butter
200 g caster sugar
1 egg yolk
500 g plain flour, sifted

Port Wine Granita
juice of 2 large oranges
    (blood oranges, when in season)
2 teaspoons caster sugar
200 ml good quality tawny or vintage port
juice of ¼ lemon

Roasted Fruits in Spiced Caramel
a selection of apples, pears,
    pineapple, strawberries,
    bananas, figs, mangoes
    (allow 4 pieces of cut fruit per person)
4 tablespoons unsalted butter
6 star anise (plus 6 extra for garnish)
3 vanilla beans, split and scraped
3 cinnamon sticks
1 liquorice root
150 g caster sugar
150 ml fresh apple juice
sprigs of mint, for garnish

Sablé Pastry
Cream the butter and sugar until pale then add the egg yolk and mix in lightly. Add the sifted flour, then scrape the pastry onto a piece of plastic film. Wrap and place in the fridge overnight (a minimum of 12 hours) until set firm.

Unwrap the pastry and place on a lightly floured work surface and roll out to a thickness of 3 mm. Cut into 6 x 15 cm circles, carefully transfer each circle to a baking tray and return to the fridge for another 3 hours.

Preheat the oven to 170°C. Bake the pastry circles for 4–5 minutes, or until a light golden colour. Remove from the oven and allow to cool.

Port Wine Granita
Heat orange juice and sugar in a medium pan until the sugar has dissolved. Bring to the boil and skim. Remove pan from the heat and stir in the port and lemon juice. Leave to cool completely then taste and add more sugar if necessary. Pour into a large deep container and freeze for a minimum of 3 hours. (If you use an ice cream machine you will achieve a smoother sorbet, rather than a granita).

Roasted Fruits in Spiced Caramel
Peel and prepare fruit; cut into large pieces. Melt butter in a heavy-based pan and add the star anise, vanilla bean and seeds, cinnamon and liquorice. Add sugar and stir until dissolved. Add the hardest fruit (pears, apples, pineapple) and cook gently for about 5 minutes, turning from time to time. Add remaining softer fruit and continue to cook gently for 3–4 minutes, until all are tender and an even golden colour. Carefully remove fruit from pan and keep warm. Deglaze pan with apple juice to make a sauce. Pour over the fruit.

To Serve
Place each shortbread base on a plate and top with a selection of roasted fruit. Drizzle with a little sauce and garnish with sprigs of fresh mint, and a star anise. Serve the granita on the side in a small chilled shot glass, drizzled with a little more port.

Serves 6

Rich and spicy by nature, with plummy fruit characters, what else but a Port would be the perfect match for this dessert?

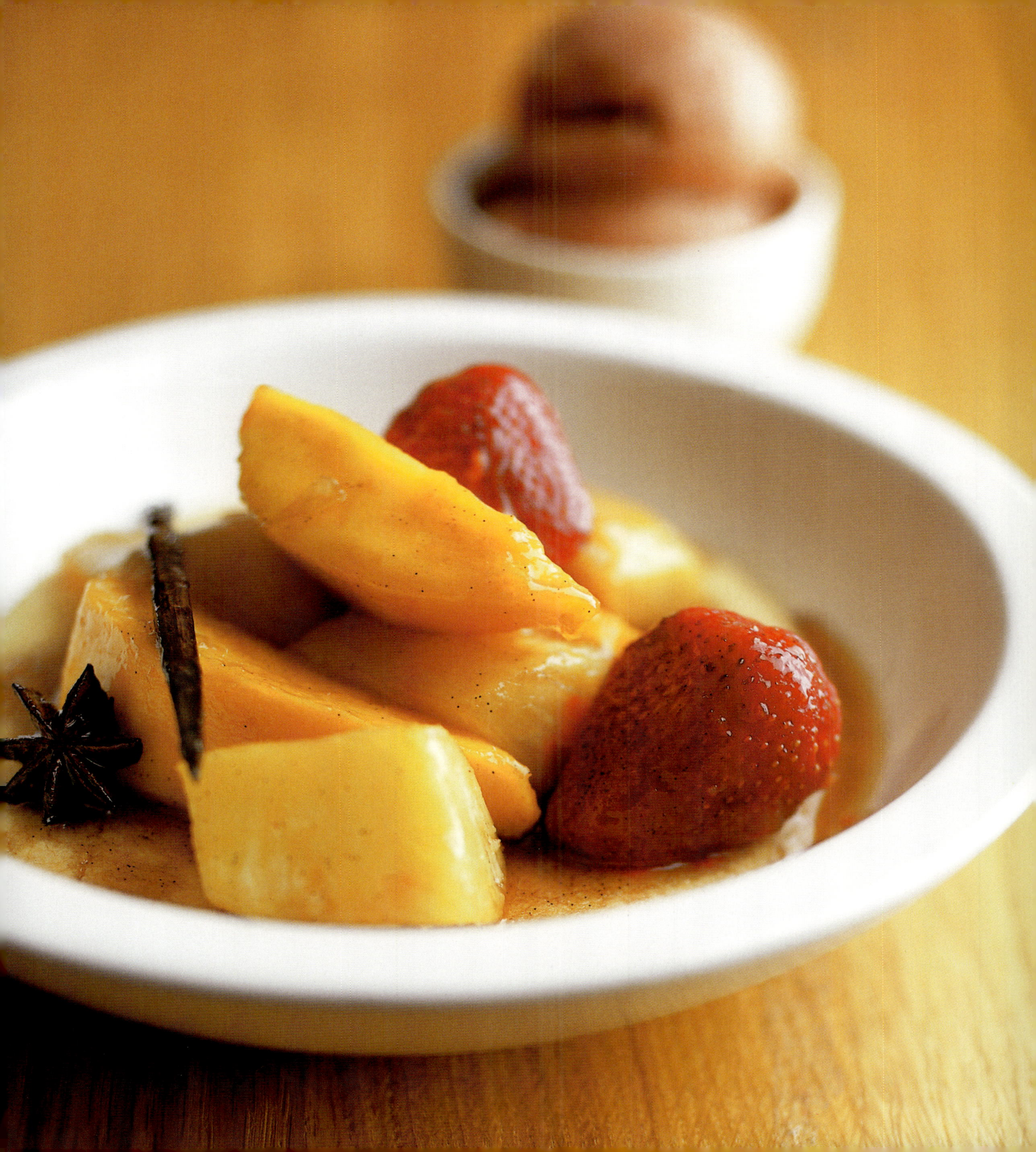

In the Hunter Valley a hot summer sun shines brightly in clear blue skies. On the vines the grapes slowly ripen. This is a time to enjoy crisp chilled white wines, salads and sorbets and a profusion of vegetables, berries and stone fruits.

summer

Olive-Fried Octopus with Avocado and Pink Grapefruit Salad

Cheong Liew

Use the giant southern octopus for this dish, which are quite different from the small Asian variety.

Olive-fried Octopus
1 litre olive oil
200 g black olives, slightly crushed
2 whole heads of garlic,
  cut in half horizontally
4 fresh chillies
2.5 kg octopus
1 bay leaf

Avocado and Pink Grapefruit Salad
2 pink grapefruit
1 Spanish onion, thinly sliced
40 g sun-dried tomatoes
2 heads frisée lettuce, separated
50 g capers
plain flour
olive oil
2 avocadoes

Dressing
3 tablespoons extra-virgin olive oil
1 clove garlic, crushed
1 tablespoon Dijon mustard
juice of 2 lemons
freshly ground black pepper
2 tablespoons dry white wine
1 teaspoon sugar

Olive-fried Octopus
Put the olive oil in a deep-fryer or a large saucepan and heat until smoking. Add the crushed olives, garlic and chillies and bring back to smoking point. Gather the octopus by the tentacles, one at a time, and lower them head first into the hot oil to seal evenly. Once they are sealed, put them all back in the oil. Add the bay leaf then cover the pan and reduce the flame to a gently simmer – as low as possible. Simmer for 45 minutes to 1 hour. Allow the octopus to cool in the oil, then remove and cut into slices. Reduce the remaining oil by one-third and set aside.

Avocado and Pink Grapefruit Salad
Peel the skin and membrane off the grapefruit. Use a sharp knife and carefully cut down each side of the membrane between each segment. Flip the segments out, removing seeds as you go. Mix together the grapefruit, onion, sun-dried tomatoes and lettuce. Roll the capers in flour and fry in the olive oil until golden brown and crispy. Set aside. Slice avocado into thin slices.

Dressing
To make the dressing, combine all the ingredients and mix with the salad.

To Serve
Arrange slices of avocado on the centre of each plate. Place slices of octopus on top of the avocado, and then a small mound of salad. Drizzle a spoonful of the octopus oil around the plate and garnish with fried capers.

Serves 6

Choose a Riesling with delicate fruit flavours that will soften the acid of the grapefruit.

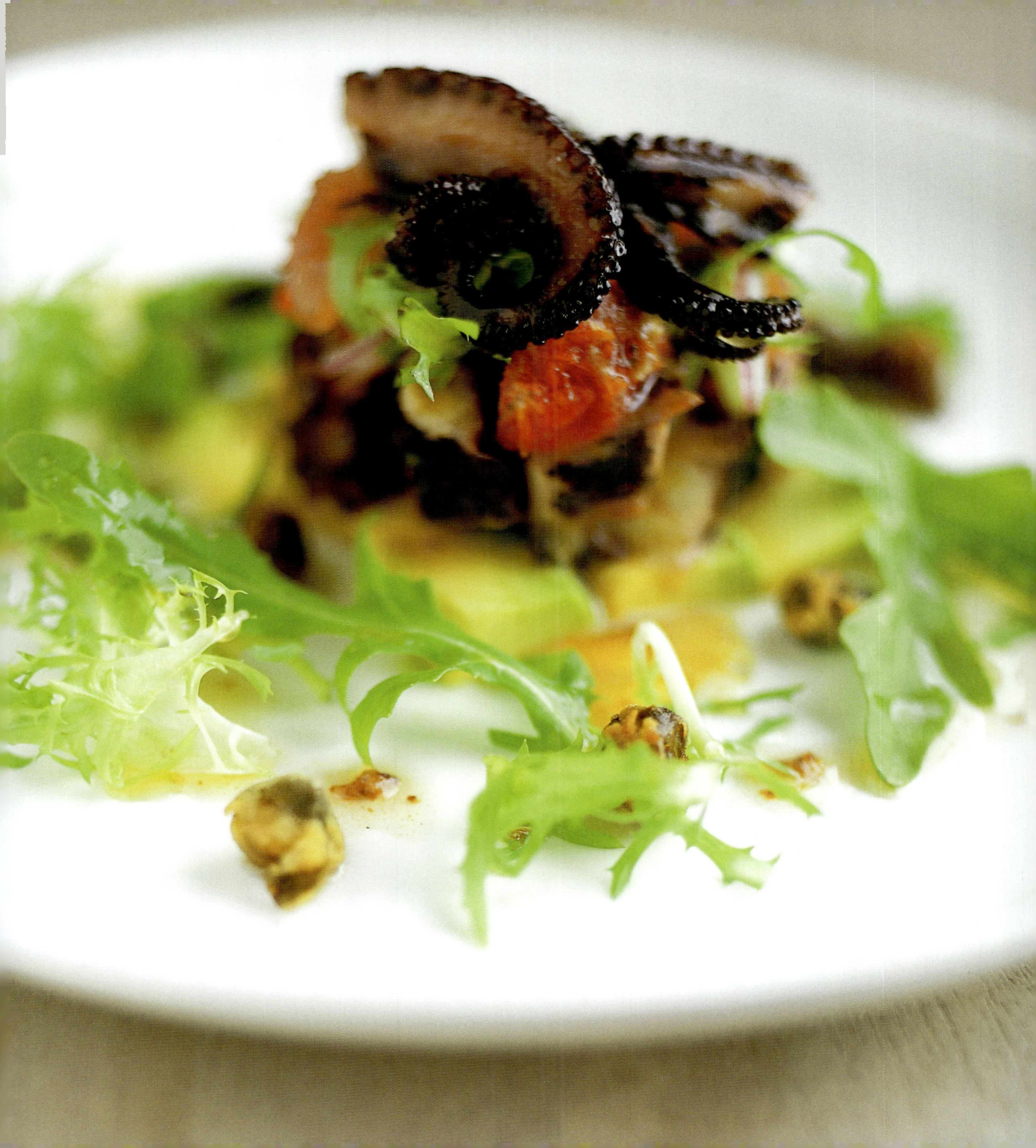

Salad of Smoked Rainbow Trout with Chardonnay Dressing

Peter Howard

300 g mixed lettuce leaves
3 medium tomatoes,
   cut into fine wedges
24 black olives
1 cup diced cucumber
3 large fillets smoked rainbow trout,
   skin and bones removed
3 hard-boiled eggs,
   shelled and cut into wedges
1 Spanish onion, cut into very fine rings
1 1/2 tablespoons chopped capers

Chardonnay Dressing
500 ml Chardonnay
150 ml extra-virgin olive oil
1 tablespoon smooth French mustard
1/2 teaspoon salt
pinch sugar

Chardonnay Dressing
Put the Chardonnay in a medium-sized pan and bring to the boil. Lower the heat and simmer until it reduces down to about 100 ml. Remove from the heat and leave to cool. Whisk together the oil, mustard, salt and sugar until lightly aerated. Slowly pour in the chardonnay and whisk gently to combine.

To Serve
Divide the lettuce leaves between 6 plates. In a large bowl, mix together the tomato wedges, olives and cucumber then scatter the mixture over the lettuce leaves. Flake the trout roughly and sprinkle it over the salad. Arrange the hard-boiled eggs and onion rings on top and scatter over the capers. Drizzle with a generous amount of dressing and serve immediately with crusty bread.

Serves 6

A Chardonnay with buttery, nutty characters will complement the richness of the smoked rainbow trout.

Poached Atlantic Salmon Salad with Tomato-Fennel Salsa

Mark Armstrong

1 whole fillet of Atlantic salmon, skinned and pin bones removed

Poaching Stock
4 sticks celery
4 medium carrots, peeled
2 onions, peeled
½ bunch of dill
6 cloves garlic
4 cloves
2 lemons
2 litres white wine
4 litres water
5 cm piece fresh ginger

Tomato-Fennel Salsa
1 medium fennel bulb
4 large ripe tomatoes, seeded
salt and pepper
50 ml extra-virgin olive oil
250 g rocket
20 ml good quality balsamic vinegar

Poaching Stock
Place all the ingredients in a large heavy-based pot and bring to the boil. Lower the heat, cover the pan and simmer for 45 minutes. Strain and pour the poaching stock back into a clean pan.

Poach the salmon in stock for 4–6 minutes. Carefully lift the salmon out of the stock, place it on a rack and leave to cool.

Tomato-Fennel Salsa
Put the whole fennel bulb in a pan with enough cold water to cover. Bring to a gentle simmer and poach until tender. Strain and leave to cool. When cool enough to handle, cut into medium-sized dice. Cut the tomatoes into similar-sized dice. Mix the fennel and tomato together, season with salt and pepper and dress with a little olive oil.

To Serve
Divide the rocket leaves between 6 plates and scatter over the tomato-fennel salsa. Break the salmon into large chunks and arrange on top of the salad. Drizzle with more olive oil and balsamic vinegar and serve straight away.

Serves 6

Frank Fol

So much has changed since my first visit to Australia. These days, Australia is leadng the world with its creative cooking, and of course, Australian wine is enjoyed everywhere too! The quality and freshness of the local produce – which is so important for me – is almost unmatched.

Widely acclaimed in his native Belgium as the 'groentenkok' (master of vegetables) Frank Fol has also earned an international reputation for his creative and imaginative dishes that he describes as a kind of avant-garde *cuisine légère*. He opened the highly regarded Sire Pynnock restaurant in Belgium's Louvain in 1989 and has been seducing diners ever since with the lightness of his food and his inventive, vegetable-based dishes. He hosts the lively cooking show *MondFol* on TV1 and is the author of five cookbooks.

Tomato Salad with Balsamic Syrup, Black Pepper and Green Pea Sorbet

This is a wonderful summer entrée that demonstrates my love of vegetables. The dish looks very pretty with bright red tomatoes and brilliant green peas. Of course you need the best quality and freshest ingredients.

6 vine-ripened tomatoes
freshly ground black pepper

Green Pea Sorbet
500 ml milk
250 g green peas
110 g sugar
5 egg yolks

Balsamic Syrup
50 g sugar
50 ml water
200 ml balsamic vinegar

Green Pea Sorbet
Bring the milk to the boil in a heavy-based saucepan then add the peas and simmer until tender. Tip into a blender and blend to a smooth purée. Push the mixture through a fine sieve and pour back into a clean pan. Slowly bring back to the boil. Meanwhile, put the sugar and egg yolks into an electric mixer and whisk at high speed until the mixture forms a thick, light foam that leaves a ribbon-like trail. Pour the boiled pea-milk slowly onto the egg mixture and whisk slowly until it is all combined. Pour through a sieve and leave to cool. When the mixture is cold, tip into an ice cream machine and churn according to the manufacturer's instructions.

Balsamic Syrup
Put the sugar in a small saucepan with the water and bring to the boil. Simmer until you get a light caramel. Add the balsamic vinegar and simmer until the syrup reduces by one-third. Leave to cool.

About 30 minutes before you serve the dish, cut the tomatoes into smallish dice. Pour on the balsamic syrup, mix gently and leave to marinate.

To Serve
Place a small mound of marinated tomatoes on each plate and top with a neat scoop of pea sorbet. Serve with plenty of freshly ground black pepper.

Serves 6

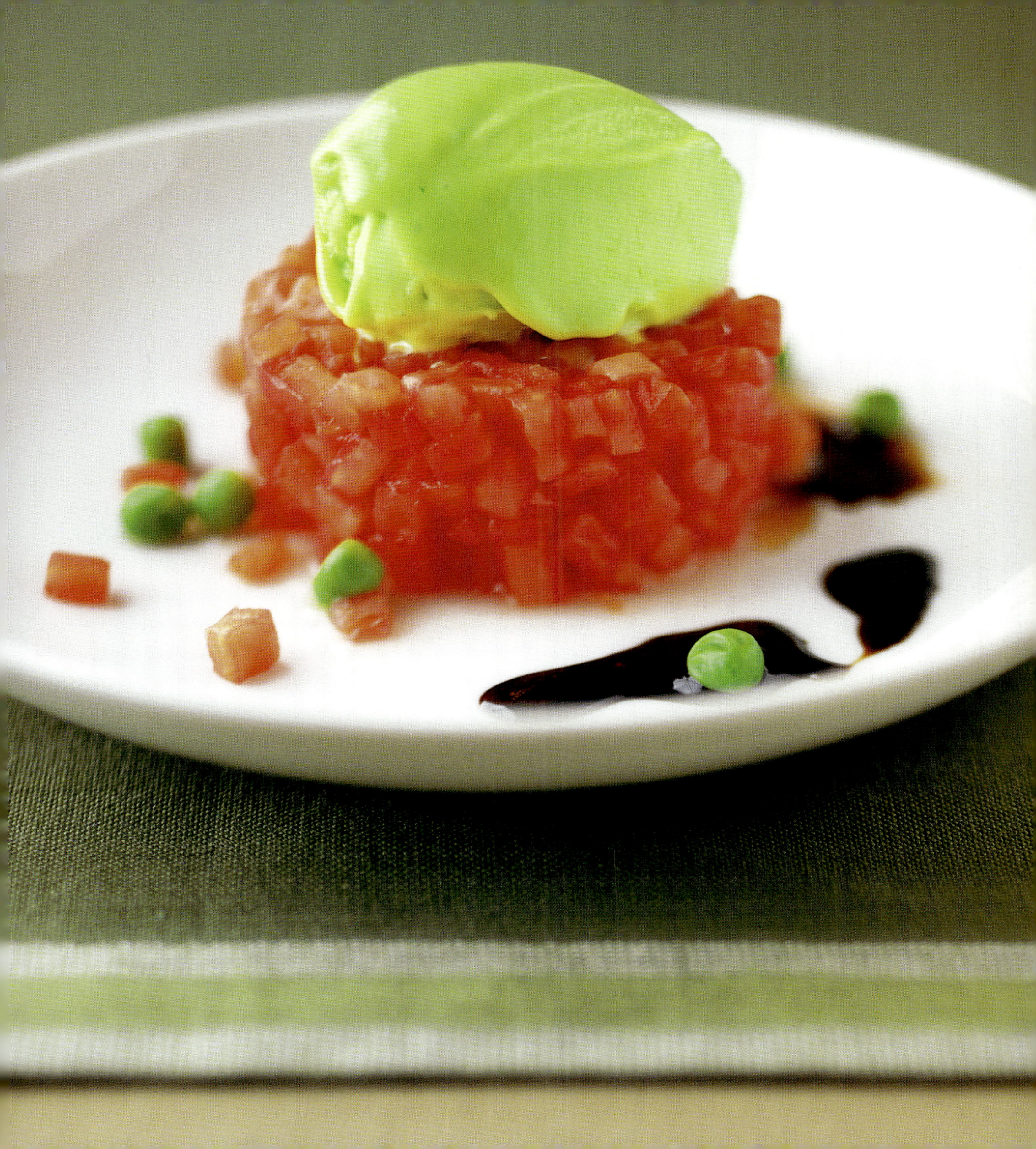

Confit of Tasmanian Salmon with a Fennel, Red Pepper and Herb Slaw

Sara Adey

Confit of Tasmanian Salmon
6 x 120 g salmon fillets,
   skin and bones removed
2–3 garlic cloves, peeled
2 sprigs thyme, roughly chopped
2 sprigs dill, roughly chopped
2 sprigs parsley, roughly chopped
2 litres olive oil

Fennel, Red Pepper and Herb Slaw
2 bulbs fennel, very finely sliced
5 spring onions, very finely sliced
2 red capsicums, roasted,
   peeled and julienned
2 tablespoons roughly chopped parsley
2 tablespoons roughly chopped basil

Dressing
1 clove garlic, crushed
3 teaspoons baby capers, well rinsed
3 anchovies
350 ml extra-virgin olive oil
100 ml walnut oil
50 ml sherry vinegar
50 ml balsamic vinegar
50 ml matsukoi (Japanese clear vinegar)
freshly ground black pepper

Confit of Tasmanian Salmon
Preheat the oven to 50°C. Fit a wire rack into the bottom of a deep baking tray. Arrange the salmon fillets on the rack, scatter in the garlic cloves and herbs and pour in the olive oil until the fish is completely immersed. Place in the oven and cook for 10–12 minutes, or until the fish is just starting to turn opaque. If it starts to turn pink and exudes a milky liquid, it is overcooked. Remove the fish from the oil, drain well and keep at room temperature until ready to serve.

Fennel, Red Pepper and Herb Slaw
To make the slaw, place the vegetables and herbs in a large mixing bowl and toss to combine.

Dressing
Place the garlic, capers and anchovies in a mortar and pound to a paste. Add the oils and mix to incorporate. Whisk in the vinegars. Lightly dress the vegetables at the last moment, reserving some dressing to drizzle over the plate.

To Serve
Place a mound of slaw in the centre of each plate and arrange a piece of confit salmon on top. Drizzle the dressing around the plate and season with plenty of freshly ground black pepper.

Serves 6

Try a light Pinot Noir with this dish, that will stand up to the strong flavours of the salmon confit.

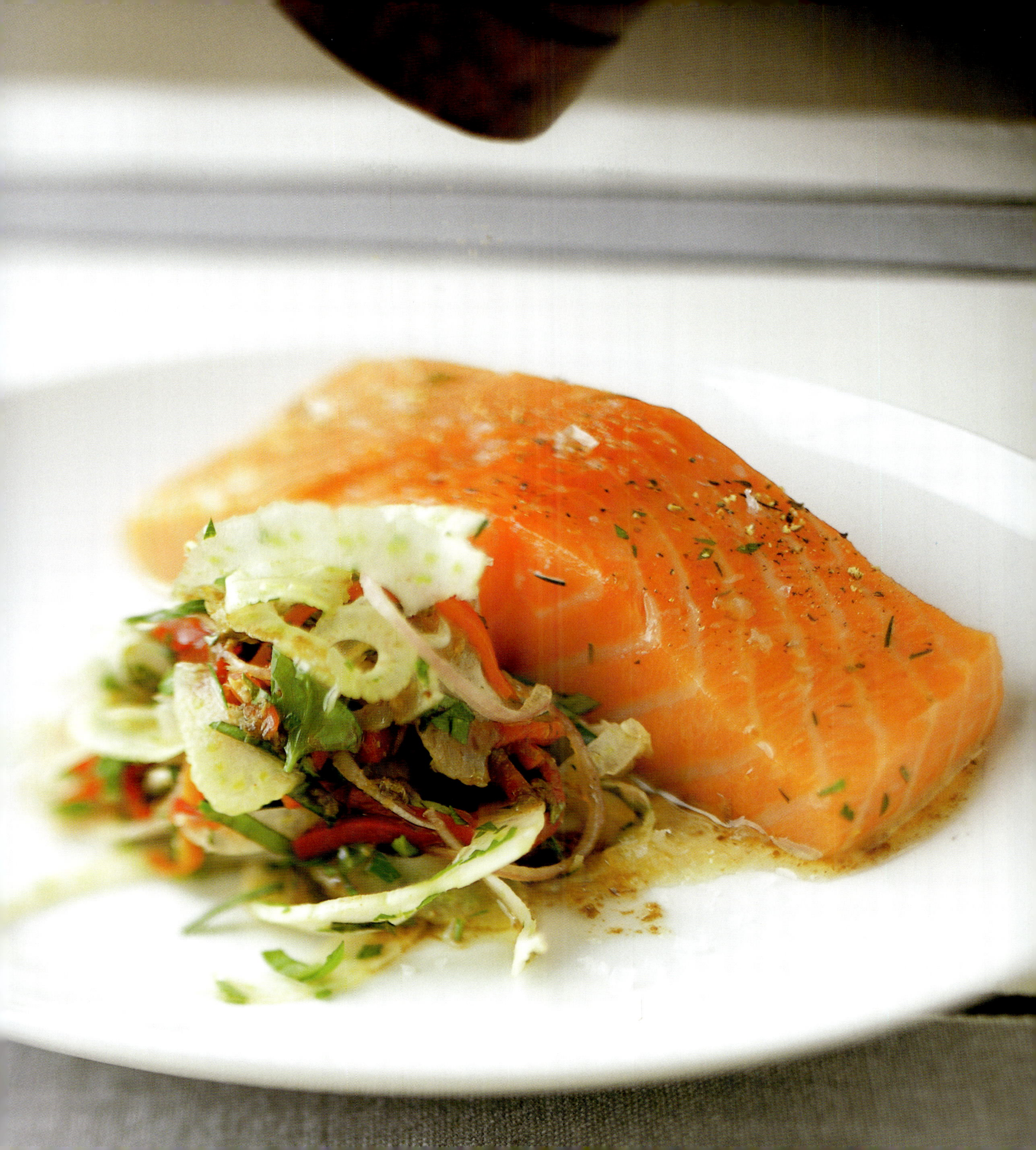

Organic Beets and Smoked Swordfish with Landcress, Dill and Horseradish-Crème Fraîche Dressing

Darren Simpson

You can get smoked swordfish from good delicatessens, but this dish works just as well with smoked salmon or smoked eel. If you can't find target beetroots, then just use a mixture of any other small variety of beetroot.

6 small golden beetroots
6 small target beetroots
6 small red beetroots
6 cloves garlic
extra-virgin olive oil
salt and freshly ground
 black pepper
1 tablespoon lemon juice
12 thin slices smoked swordfish
a generous handful of landcress
 (or watercress or rocket leaves)

Horseradish-Crème Fraîche Dressing
2 tablespoons freshly grated horseradish
6 tablespoons crème fraîche
2 teaspoons finely chopped dill
2 teaspoons French mustard
salt and freshly ground black pepper

Preheat the oven to 180°C. Scrub the beetroots under cold running water. Leave the tops and trimmed roots attached. Place the beetroots in a small roasting tin with the garlic. Drizzle with olive oil and add a splash of water to the tin. Season with salt and pepper, cover with aluminium foil and roast in the oven for around 30 minutes, or until tender. Test for doneness by piercing with the sharp point of a knife. Remove the beetroots from the tin and carefully peel away the skins.

While the beetroots are still warm, whisk together 6 tablespoons extra-virgin olive oil and the lemon juice and dress the beetroots so that all are lightly coated. Season with salt and pepper.

Horseradish-Crème Fraîche Dressing
Place all the ingredients in a mixing bowl and stir well to combine. Season with salt and pepper to taste.

To Serve
Divide the beetroots between each plate. Arrange a few slices of smoked swordfish on each plate and a dollop of horseradish-crème fraîche dressing. Garnish with landcress and serve straight away.

Serves 6

Try a Verdelho with this starter. The fresh tropical-fruit salad flavours will complement the sweetness of the beetroot, and balance the savoury richness of the smoked fish and dressing.

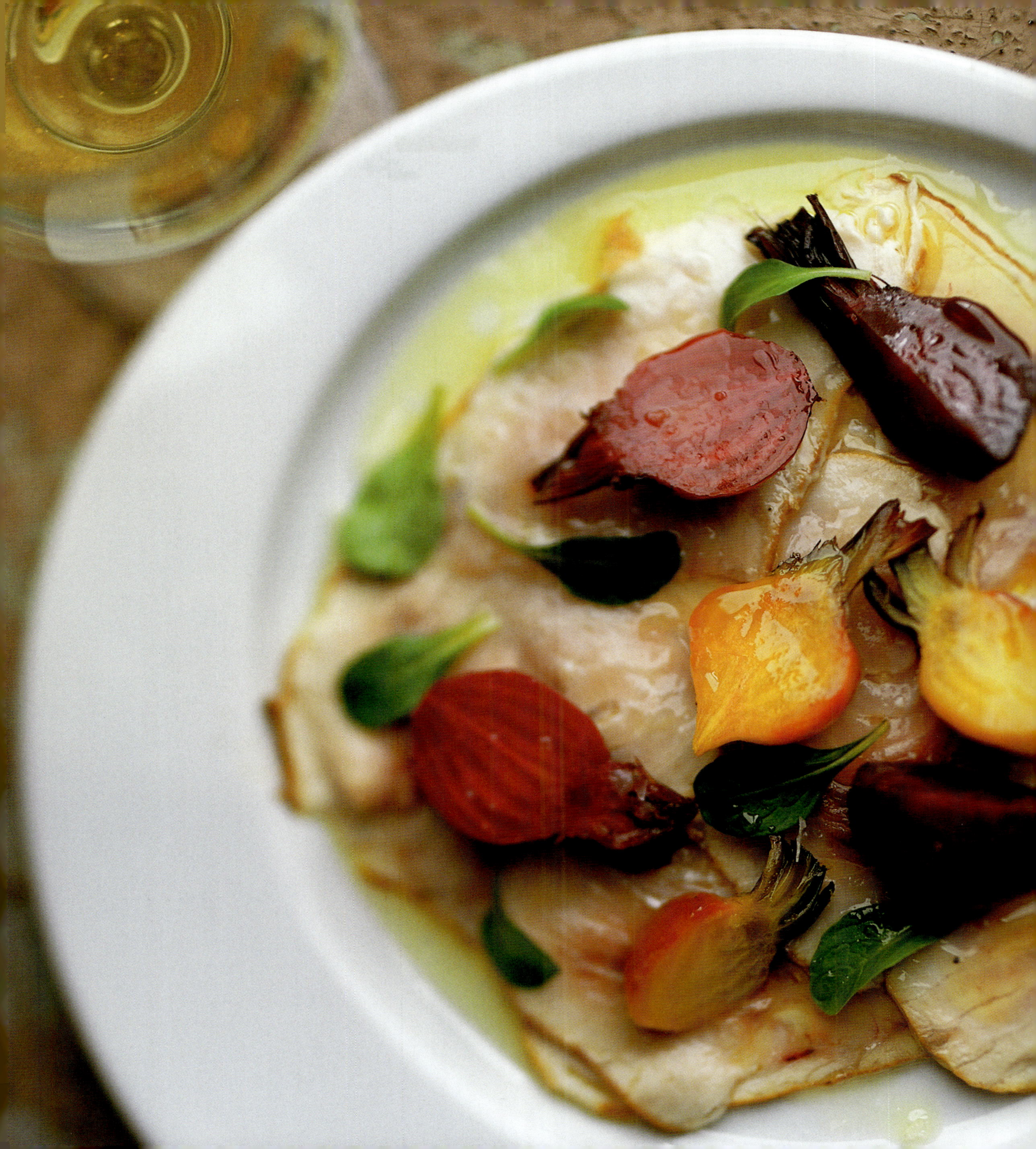

Striped Marlin Loin with Cardamom Sauce, Spicy Potatoes and Peas

Tony Papas

6 x 200 g pieces marlin loin,
   bloodline removed
100 ml ghee or clarified butter
salt and pepper

Cardamom Sauce
2.5 cm piece fresh ginger,
   peeled and pounded to a paste
2 cloves garlic, peeled and
   pounded to a paste
2 tablespoons olive oil
1/2 teaspoon chilli powder
1/2 teaspoon salt
350 g onions, finely chopped
1 tablespoon turmeric powder
1 tablespoon black cardamon seeds,
   removed from the husks
1 tablespoon cardamom seeds,
   removed from the husks
3 bay leaves
1/2 teaspoon asafoetida*
1 teaspoon fenugreek*
1 tablespoon ground fennel seeds
1 tablespoon ground cumin seeds
180 ml fish stock
75 ml malt vinegar
2 tablespoons palm sugar

Spicy Potatoes and Peas
40 ml vegetable oil
3 tablespoons sliced garlic
3 tablespoons sliced shallots
3 teaspoons sliced red chillies
1 teaspoon ghee or clarified butter
2 teaspoons split black dhal
2 tablespoons unsalted butter
500 g large kipfler potatoes, cooked,
   peeled and cut in half lengthwise
250 g fresh green peas,
   cooked until tender
100 g fresh grated coconut
50 ml lime juice

Cardamom Sauce

Fry the ginger and garlic pastes in a dry pan for a few moments. Add the olive oil, chilli powder, salt and onions. Sauté over a very low heat until the mixture turns a light golden brown and the onions soften. Add remaining spices and herbs and sauté for a further 5 minutes to release the flavours. Add the fish stock and simmer on a low heat for 1 hour. Add the vinegar and sugar and simmer for a further 15 minutes.

Spicy Potatoes and Peas

Heat the vegetable oil in a frying pan and fry the garlic, shallots and chillies until they are lightly browned. Be careful not to burn them or they will taste bitter. Remove from the pan and drain. Heat the ghee and fry the dhal until it turns a nut-brown colour. Remove from the pan and drain on absorbent paper. Melt the unsalted butter and add the potatoes and peas. Sauté until they are warmed through. Keep until ready to serve.

To prepare the marlin, heat the ghee or butter in a large heavy-based frying pan. Season the marlin with salt and pepper and fry quickly on each side to colour. Add the hot cardamom sauce and allow to bubble for a few moments. Remove the pan from the heat and leave for 3–4 minutes to allow the fish to warm through – it should be medium-rare, not cooked right through.

Just before you are ready to serve, put the fried garlic, shallots, chillies and the toasted dhal in a large mixing bowl and add the fresh coconut and lime juice to taste. Toss to combine and sprinkle this 'tempering' mix over the warm potatoes and peas.

To Serve

Arrange a spoonful of the potatoes and peas in the centre of each plate and top with a piece of marlin. Spoon over a generous amount of sauce and serve straight away.

Serves 6

*Note: Asafoetida is a resinous gum from a species of giant fennel. It may be bought as a gum or powder and has a pungent, garlicky quality. It is used in Indian cuisine, particularly in regions where the local faith prohibits the eating of garlic.

Fenugreek seeds are also used in Indian curries, where they add a distinctive sharp, spicy and almost bitter flavour.

Corn-Fed Spatchcock with Indonesian Sweetcorn Fritters and Coriander Pesto

Sara Adey

Both the coriander pesto and corn fritter batter may be prepared in advance.

6 x 500 g corn-fed spatchcocks
2 tablespoons olive oil
½ cup baby coriander leaves to garnish

Marinade
2 bay leaves
2 cloves garlic, sliced
1 cup coriander leaves, chopped
2 tablespoons finely chopped lemongrass
1 long red chilli, finely sliced
1 tablespoon harissa paste

Coriander Pesto
120 ml extra-virgin olive oil
1 ¼ cups chopped coriander
   (leaves and stalks)
1 cup parsley leaves, chopped
1 tablespoon grated parmesan cheese
4 garlic chives, chopped
1 small clove garlic, chopped
¼ cup macadamia nuts, toasted

Indonesian Corn Fritters
2 cloves garlic, finely chopped
¼ cup celery leaves, finely chopped
½ teaspoon chilli powder
½ teaspoon paprika
½ teaspoon ground coriander
1 egg
½ cup plain flour
2 tablespoons potato flour
¼ cup coconut milk
1 ½ cups cooked corn kernels
olive oil for frying

Marinade
Combine all the ingredients in a large mixing bowl. Rub the marinade into the spatchcock and refrigerate for a minimum of 2 hours, or overnight.

Coriander Pesto
Place half the olive oil in a blender with the remaining ingredients and blend until smooth and well incorporated. With the motor running slowly, pour in the remaining oil and process until smooth. If the mixture seems too thick, add a little more oil.

Indonesian Corn Fritters
Put the garlic and celery leaves in a blender or processor and blend with the chilli powder, paprika and coriander until well incorporated. In a large bowl, combine the egg, flours and coconut milk until a smooth batter. Add the garlic-spice paste and corn kernels and mix well. If making ahead of time, cover and refrigerate until needed. If the mixture thickens, thin it with a little more coconut milk.

Heat a little oil in a large frying pan. Drop large spoonfuls of batter into the oil to form fritters, about 8 cm in diameter. The batter makes about 6 fritters, so aim to cook 3 at a time. Fry for a couple of minutes on each side, until golden brown and cooked through. Keep warm while you fry the remaining fritters and
eat as soon as possible.

Corn-fed Spatchcock
Preheat the oven to 200°C. Heat the oil in a large, heavy-based, ovenproof pan. Brown the spatchcocks well on all sides. Transfer the pan to the oven and roast for 10 minutes, or until cooked through. Remove from the oven and rest in a warm place for 5 minutes before cutting each spatchcock into quarters.

To Serve
Place a fritter in the centre of each plate and arrange the quartered spatchcock on top. Spoon on a generous dollop of pesto and serve immediately.

Serves 6

Try a Grenache. The chalky structure with fresh berry fruit flavours will be an interesting match with the components of this dish.

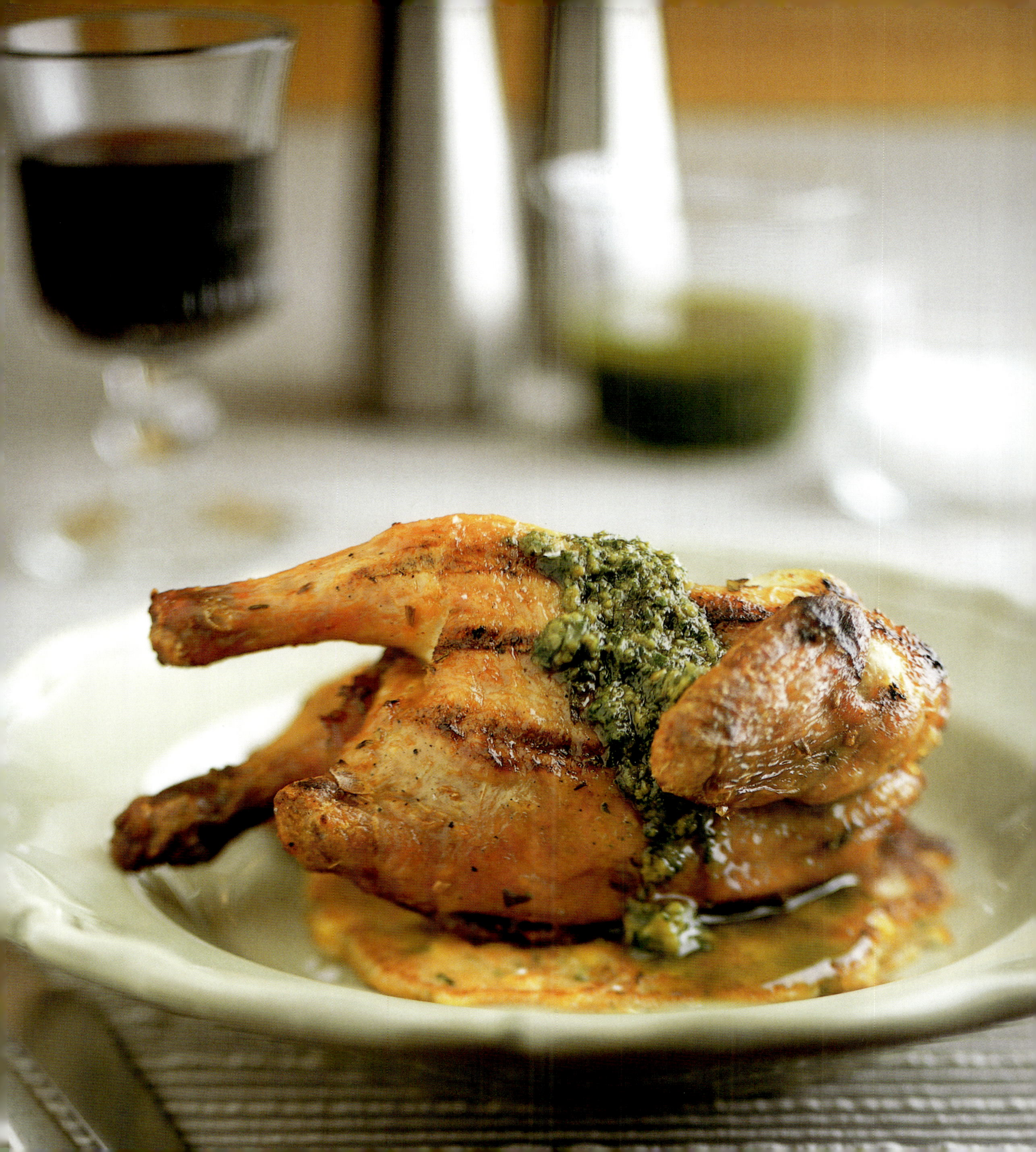

Darren Simpson

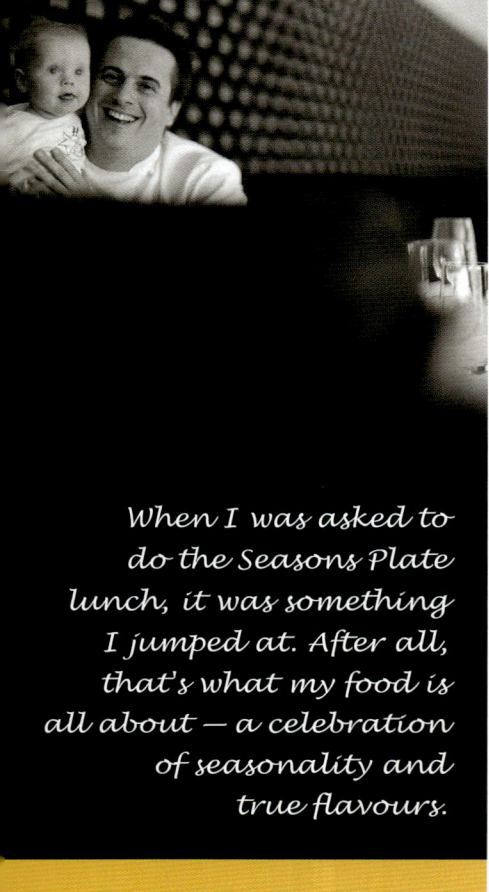

When I was asked to do the Seasons Plate lunch, it was something I jumped at. After all, that's what my food is all about — a celebration of seasonality and true flavours.

Northern Irish-born chef Darren Simpson began his career working with some of Europe's most highly regarded chefs, including Albert Roux and Simon Hopkinson. He was named Young Chef of the Year at age 21 and at age 27 was appointed head chef at Sir Terence Conran's Sartoria restaurant. In more recent years Darren has been wowing diners at Sydney's modern Italian restaurant, Aqua Luna. His food is deceptively simple, and features the pure flavours and quality seasonal ingredients of the best Italian cooking.

Roasted Ribeye of Free-Range Veal with Garlic, Coppa, Rosemary, Capers, Parsley and Mustard

To make life easy, ask your butcher to remove the veal loin from the rib bones for you.

Roasted Ribeye of Veal
1 x 2 kg veal ribeye, bones removed
2 cloves garlic, finely sliced
20 g prosciutto fat, cut into small strips
small sprigs rosemary
250 g caul fat (see p 115), soaked in cold salted water for 1 hour
12 thin slices coppa or pancetta
salt and freshly ground black pepper
3 tablespoons olive oil
100 ml good quality red wine (an Italian Chianti would be perfect)
150 ml home-made veal or chicken stock

Dressing
100 g stale white bread
2 tablespoons capers, chopped
2 tablespoons French mustard
2 tablespoons finely chopped parsley
1 teaspoon finely chopped tarragon
120 ml extra-virgin olive oil
2 tablespoons herb vinegar

Vegetable Garnish
220 g cavolo nero (Italian kale)
4 tablespoons extra-virgin olive oil
1 clove garlic, finely sliced
salt and pepper
12 asparagus spears

Roasted Ribeye of Veal
Preheat the oven to 210°C. Use the point of a sharp kitchen knife to make small incisions all over the veal loin. Stud with slivers of garlic, prosciutto fat and small sprigs of rosemary. Drain the caul fat well and pat dry. Carefully spread it out on a work surface. Lay the slices of coppa on top of the caul fat then place the veal loin on top. Roll the caul fat up and around the veal, so it is encased in a layer of coppa, held in by the caul. Trim away any excess. Season lightly all over with salt and pepper.

Seal the veal loin in the olive oil so it is evenly browned then transfer to the oven and roast for 25 minutes until medium-rare. Remove from the oven and leave in a warm place for 10 minutes to rest. Deglaze the baking tray with the red wine and simmer until reduced to a few tablespoons. Add the stock and simmer briefly, skimming away any fat if necessary. Taste and adjust seasoning. Pass through a fine sieve and keep sauce warm until ready to serve.

Dressing
Soak the bread briefly under running water then squeeze dry. Pound to a paste using a mortar and pestle, then scrape into a food processor with the other ingredients. Pulse in short bursts until blended.

Vegetable Garnish
Wash the cavolo nero, remove the large stems and discard. Blanch the leaves in boiling salted water, until tender. Heat half the the extra-virgin olive oil in a large pan and fry the garlic until a light golden colour. Add the cavolo nero, toss well in the oil, season with salt and pepper and remove from the heat.

Preheat a griddle or barbecue. Peel the asparagus and snap off the woody ends. Brush with the remaining olive oil and grill for 3–5 minutes, or until tender, turning so they brown evenly. (Alternatively, roast in a hot oven for about 5 minutes, tossing from time to time.)

To Serve
Slice the veal thickly and top with a dollop of dressing. Serve with the cavolo nero and asparagus spears and drizzle the plate with a little sauce.

Serves 6

Choose a soft, silky Merlot with generous fruit flavours to complement the robust flavours in this dish.

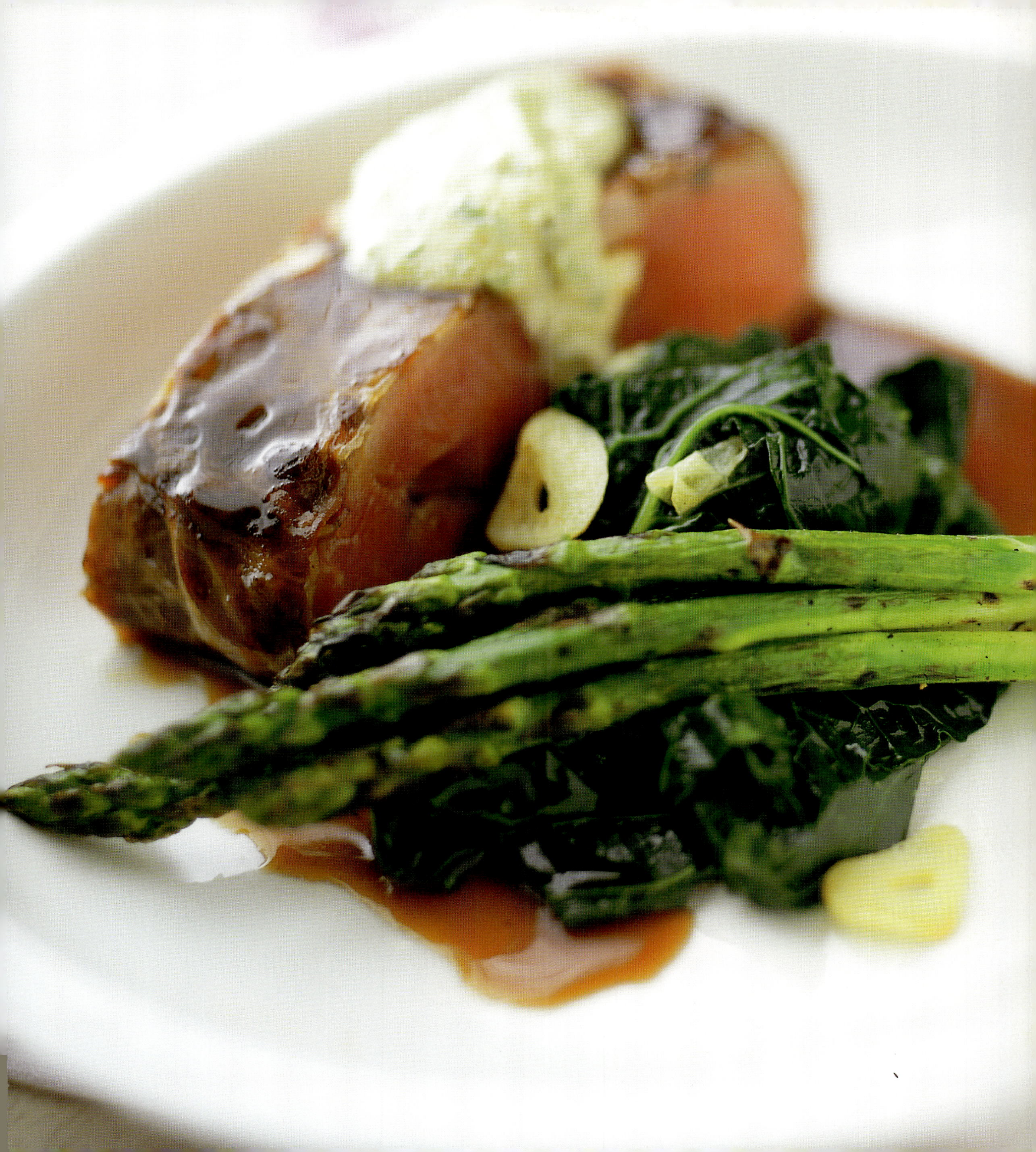

Noisettes of Lamb with Carrot Purée and a Warm Summer Vegetable Salad

Frank Fol

12 x 60 g lamb noisettes (2 per person)
olive oil
salt and pepper
300 ml lamb stock
a few sprigs of thyme

Carrot Purée
300 g carrots, scraped and
 roughly chopped
1 large onion, roughly chopped
2 potatoes, peeled and cut into chunks
1 bay leaf
2 sprigs thyme, plus extra to garnish
½ teaspoon salt
50 g butter

Parsley Oil
2 cups parsley leaves
a few sprigs of thyme, leaves only
100 ml olive oil
50 ml vegetable stock
salt and pepper

Warm Summer Vegetable Salad
200 g thin green beans
2 carrots, cut into 1 cm dice
2 cooked artichoke hearts
40 ml olive oil
a splash of white wine vinegar

Carrot Purée
Put the carrots in a large saucepan with the onion and potatoes. Cover with cold water and add the herbs and salt. Bring to the boil and cook until all the vegetables are tender. Remove the herbs and drain the vegetables, reserving some of the cooking water to make a sauce for the lamb. Tip into a blender, add the butter and blend to a smooth purée.

Parsley Oil
Blanch the parsley and thyme leaves in boiling water for 30 seconds. Refresh in cold water and squeeze dry. Put the herbs in a blender with the olive oil, vegetable stock, salt and pepper. Blend to a very smooth purée. Pour the mixture into a chinois or fine sieve lined with muslin and leave to drain overnight. The parsley oil can be made in advance. It stores well for 5 days.

Warm Summer Vegetable Salad
Blanch and refresh the green beans. Cook the carrots until they are just tender. Dice the cooked artichoke hearts. When you are ready to serve, heat the olive oil in a large frying pan and add the vegetables. Cook gently until just warmed through. Add the vinegar and stir.

Noisettes of Lamb
Heat the olive oil in a heavy-based frying pan. Cook the lamb noisettes for 3 minutes on each side for medium-rare, or until cooked to your liking. Season with salt and pepper and keep warm while you make the sauce. Deglaze the pan with the lamb stock and some of the reserved carrot water. Add the thyme and simmer for a few minutes to make a sauce.

To Serve
Place 2 lamb noisettes in the middle of each plate and pour over a little sauce. Spoon a quenelle of carrot purée to one side of the lamb and top with a sprig of thyme. Arrange a small mound of warm vegetable salad on top of the lamb. Drizzle some parsley oil around the plate and serve straight away.

Serves 6

Shiraz has the spiciness and body to match the stronger flavours of the lamb and vegetables in this dish.

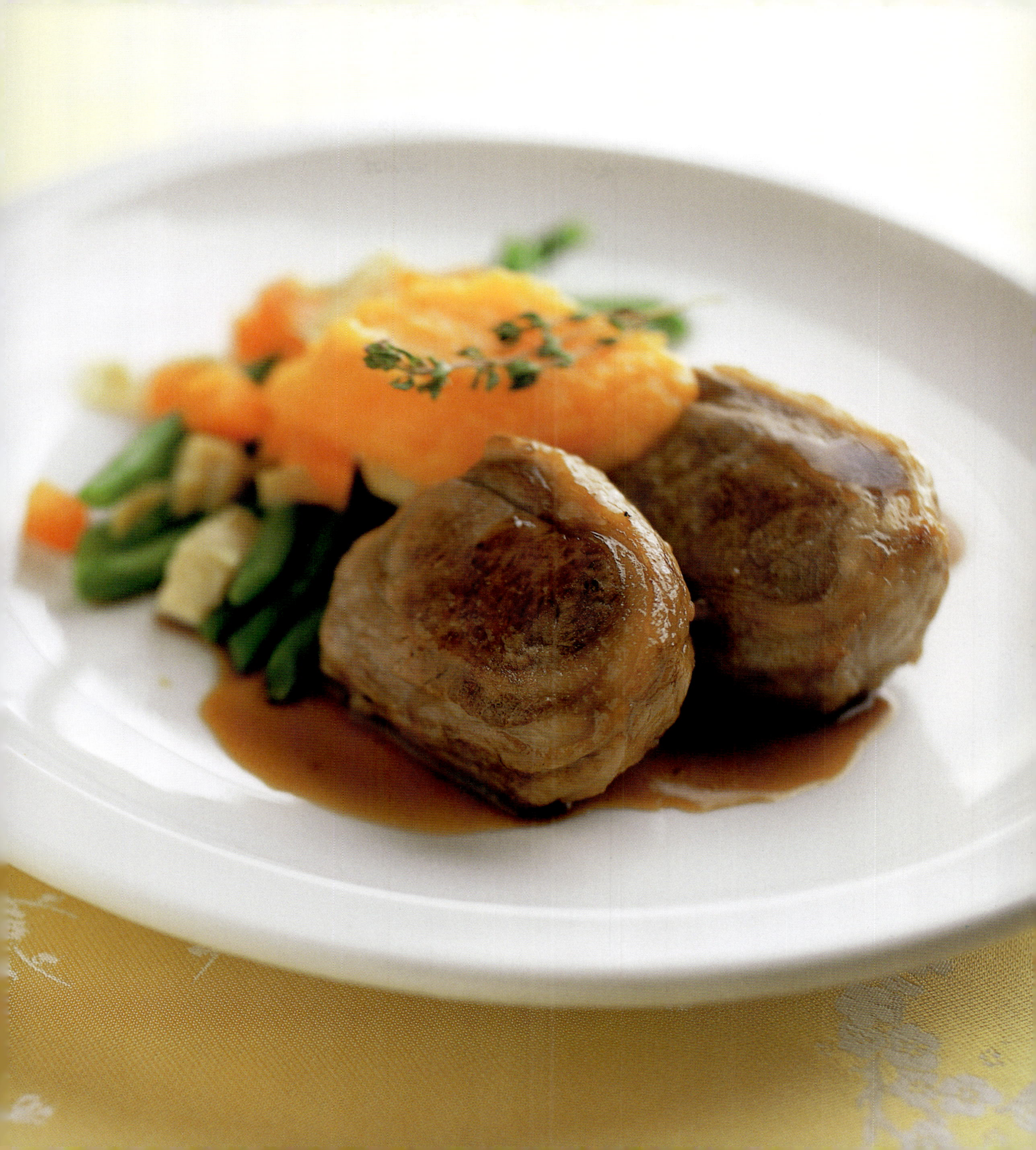

Beef Brisket and Beef Tenderloin with Mushroom Confit and Creamy Potato

Serge Dansereau

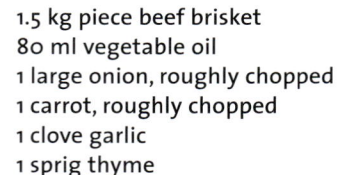

1.5 kg piece beef brisket
80 ml vegetable oil
1 large onion, roughly chopped
1 carrot, roughly chopped
1 clove garlic
1 sprig thyme
3 bay leaves
salt and ground pepper
cold water to cover
1 kg beef tenderloin

Mushroom Confit
6 open field mushrooms (12 cm diameter)
2 sprigs thyme
2 cloves garlic, sliced
150 ml walnut or olive oil
salt and ground black pepper

Creamy Potato
500 g desirée potatoes
   (or another good mashing variety)
100 g cold butter, diced
100 ml cream or milk, warmed
salt and pepper

Preheat the oven to 175°C. To cook the beef brisket, heat the oil in heavy-based pot and sear the beef on a high heat until well-coloured all over. Drain off excess oil then add the vegetables, garlic, herbs, salt and pepper. Pour on cold water, cover with lid and braise in the oven for 3 hours. Allow to cool in the stock. When cool, remove the beef brisket and shred into long strands, taking care to remove any fat or gristle. Reserve the stock.

For the sauce, strain the stock into a saucepan and simmer until reduced. If the sauce becomes too thick, add a glass of red wine and simmer again until you have the right consistency. Strain through a very fine sieve and set aside until ready to serve.

To cook the beef tenderloin, preheat the oven to 180°C. Roast the beef tenderloin to your liking, around 1 hour for medium-rare. Remove from the oven and leave in a warm place to rest for 10 minutes. When ready to serve, slice to finger thickness.

Mushroom Confit
Preheat the oven to 150°C. Trim the stalks and flaps of the mushrooms then place them, gills facing up, on a shallow oven tray. Sprinkle with thyme, garlic and oil and season. Cook for 1 hour, basting frequently. Remove from the oven, discard the thyme and garlic and drain off excess oil and juices. Set aside.

Creamy Potato
Drop the potatoes into a large pan of cold salted water, bring to the boil and cook until soft. Purée through a rice mill or use a hand masher until they are smooth. Add the cold butter, mix well and adjust seasoning. Just before serving, gradually stir in the warm cream or milk until you achieve the right consistency.

To Serve
When ready to serve, place the shredded brisket in a large pan, and warm through very slowly, moistened with a small amount of sauce.

To present this dish perfectly, use a metal ring mould or piece of plastic tube 9–10 cm diameter and 6 cm high. Place the ring on top of each mushroom and cut into a perfect round with a small sharp knife. Place the ring in the centre of each plate and fill with 2 cm of creamy potato. Top with 3 cm of the beef brisket and carefully lift off the ring. Top each neat mound with a mushroom and then a slice of beef tenderloin. Drizzle a little sauce around the plate and serve straight away.

Serves 6

Roast Fillet of Beef with Mushroom Risotto Cake and Mushroom Ragoût

Peter Howard

The mushroom risotto cake may be made the day before you plan to serve it. It needs to be refrigerated for at least 6 hours.

1 x 1.5 kg fillet of beef (from the butt end)
2 tablespoons olive oil
salt and pepper

Mushroom Stock
200 g white mushrooms
   (i.e. shameji, oneki)
1 teaspoon butter
80 ml white wine
juice of ½ lemon
salt and pepper
1 litre water
sprig thyme
2 bay leaves

Mushroom Risotto Cake
60 ml olive oil
30 g butter
1 medium onion, finely diced
250 g arborio rice
100 g grated parmesan
1 tablespoon finely chopped parsley
salt and freshly ground white pepper
extra olive oil for frying

Mushroom Ragoût
30 g butter
60 g chopped spring onions
3 cloves garlic, minced
300 g assorted mushrooms
600 ml reduced beef stock
60 ml red wine
freshly chopped marjoram

Mushroom Stock
Melt the butter in a saucepan and sauté the mushrooms until they soften. Add the wine and lemon juice, salt and pepper, cover with a lid and sauté for a further 5 minutes. Add the water, thyme and bay leaves and simmer gently for 20 minutes. Remove the mushrooms from the stock, dice them finely and reserve. Keep the mushroom stock simmering.

Mushroom Risotto Cake
Heat oil and butter in a large heavy-based pan. Add onion and cook for 2 minutes. Add rice and stir for 2 minutes to coat each grain with oil. Add a third of the simmering stock and cook on medium heat, stirring from time to time, until most of stock has been absorbed. Add another third of stock and continue cooking and stirring until it has been absorbed. Add diced mushrooms with remaining stock and stir gently until nearly all the stock has been absorbed then stir in the parmesan and parsley and season with salt and pepper. Cover and allow to rest off the heat for a few minutes. Tip risotto into an oiled 20 cm spring-form tin. Cover and when cool, put in refrigerator for at least 6 hours.

Mushroom Ragoût
Heat butter in a heavy-based pan. Add spring onions and garlic and cook for 2 minutes. Add mushrooms, stock and red wine and bring to the boil. Lower heat and simmer for an hour; add the marjoram and simmer for an additional 10 minutes.

Roast Fillet of Beef
Preheat the oven to 200°C. Heat the oil in a heavy-based ovenproof dish. Sear the beef so that it colours all over. Transfer to the oven and roast for 20–25 minutes, turning halfway through the cooking time. Remove from the oven and allow to rest for 15 minutes before slicing.

To Serve
Cut the risotto cake into 6–8 wedges and brush with olive oil. Fry or grill wedges until they are crisp and golden on the outside, but still creamy inside. Arrange a wedge on each plate and put beef slices over the pointed end. Spoon some mushroom ragoût onto the beef and serve with steamed green vegetables.

Serves 6

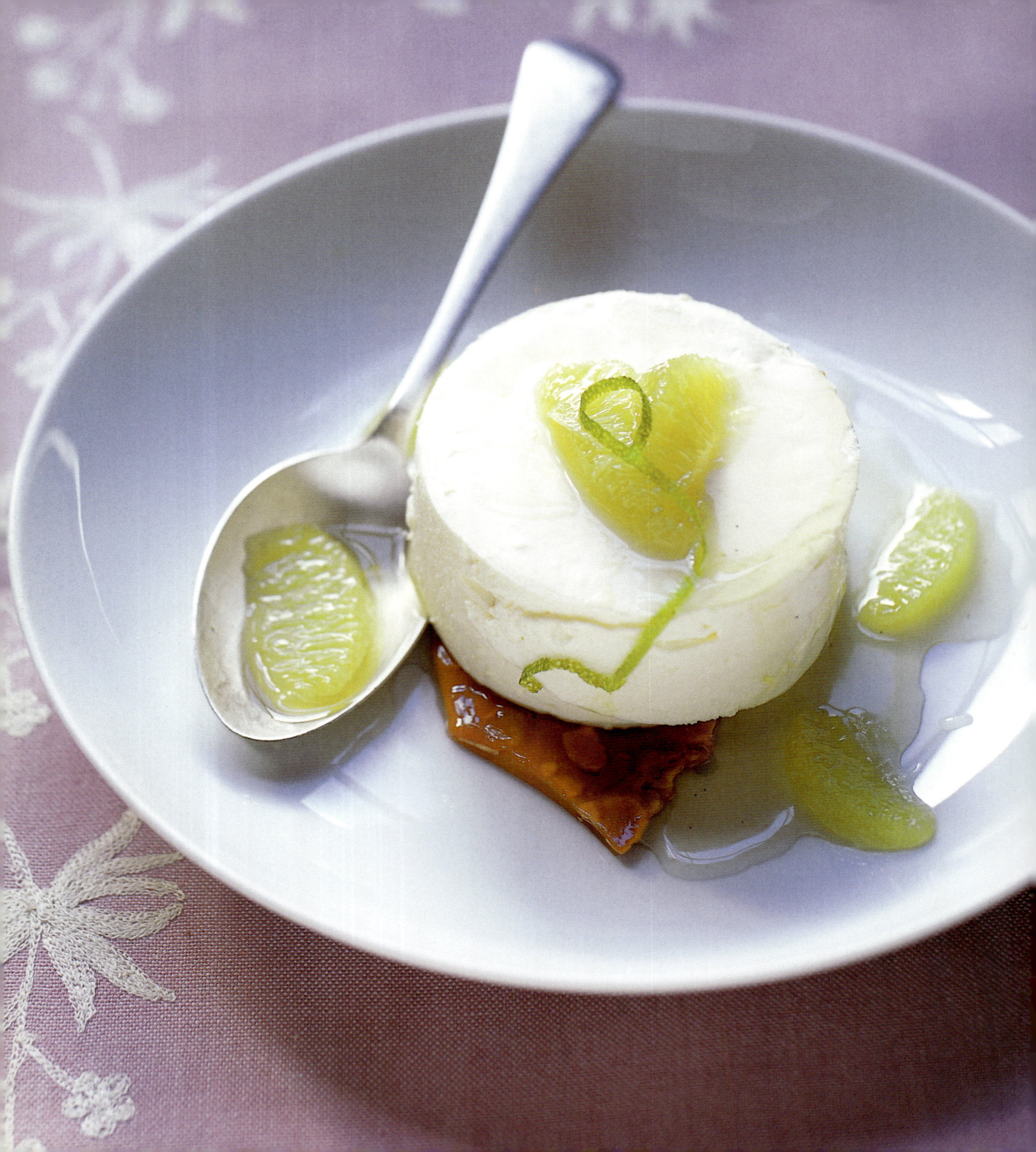

Fromage Blanc Tart with Lime Compote and Nougatine

The quantities make 12 tarts, but it is best to make this amount as the recipe works better.

Fromage Blanc Tarts
135 g caster sugar
85 ml water
4 egg yolks
8 leaves gelatine
20 ml sugar syrup
335 g cream cheese, softened
zest of ½ lime
1 litre pouring cream, whipped softly

Lime Compote
5 limes, zested and segmented, zest reserved
200 g caster sugar
65 ml lime juice
200 ml water

Nougatine
135 g flaked almonds
220 g caster sugar
20 g butter, softened

Fromage Blanc Tarts

Place the caster sugar and water in a heavy-based saucepan and stir over a moderate heat until the sugar dissolves. Boil without stirring until the mixture caramelises and reaches the soft-ball stage (116°C) on a candy thermometer. Allow to cool slightly.

Meanwhile, whisk the egg yolks in a processor until thickened and pale. With the motor running, slowly pour the syrup onto the eggs. Continue whisking until the mixture cools and forms thick ribbons.

Soak the gelatine leaves in cold water for a few minutes, then squeeze out excess water. Place the gelatine leaves in a small pan with the 20 ml sugar syrup and stir over a gentle heat until dissolved. Allow to cool.

Combine the cream cheese and lime zest. Fold the cream cheese into the egg yolk mixture with the gelatine. Fold in the softly whipped cream. Mix well until smooth.

Wet the inside of ring moulds (10 cm diameter x 4 cm high), and place them on a tray lined with waxed paper. Pour in the mixture and refrigerate overnight.

Lime Compote

Place the lime zest in boiling water for 5 minutes, then strain and run under cold water. Repeat 3 times. Place the caster sugar in a dry saucepan and cook over a moderate heat, stirring, until it turns a light gold colour. Add the lime juice and water and cook over a gentle heat until reduced by three-quarters. Skim from time to time. Remove from the heat and allow to cool. Add the lime segments and the blanched lime zest.

Nougatine

Preheat the oven to 170°C. Scatter the almonds on a baking tray and bake until lightly toasted. Place the sugar in a saucepan and stir over a gentle heat until it turns golden. Stir in the almonds and butter. Allow to cool a little then pour out onto an oiled work surface and roll with an oiled rolling pin to a 2 mm thickness.

To Serve

Place the ring moulds of fromage blanc on top of the nougatine. With a sharp, flexible knife cut around the sides of the ring mould, through the nougatine, dipping in hot water from time to time. Carefully lift off the ring mould and use a wide spatula to transfer each tart to a dessert plate. Drizzle with lime compote and serve.

Serves 12

Serge Dansereau

For all of my working life as a chef in Australia I have dedicated myself to seeking out small producers. To have the opportunity of working with people that have firm links to the food and wine regions of this amazing country is a great joy.

Serge Dansereau was born in Canada and trained at the prestigious Institut de Tourisme et d'Hôtellerie in Quebec. In 1983 he was invited to Sydney to launch Kables restaurant at the Regent Hotel where he earned high praise and three Chef's Hats. In 1999 Serge moved to another landmark Sydney restaurant, The Bather's Pavilion, as co-owner and chef. He is the author of *Food and Friends*, and is a recipient of the *Sydney Morning Herald* Special Award for Excellence for 'his work in helping redefine Australian cuisine'.

Sauterne Jelly with Fresh Strawberries and Honey Sabayon

Tony Papas

Sauterne Jelly
450 ml sauterne
60 g caster sugar
5 small leaves gelatine (8.5 g), soaked in cold water to soften
120 ml champagne

Strawberries
500 g strawberries, plus 6 extra large strawberries
1 tablespoon caster sugar

Honey Sabayon
4 egg yolks
1 heaped tablespoon caster sugar
50 g honey
100 ml apple juice
75 ml softly whipped cream

Sauterne Jelly
Put a third of the sauterne in a heavy-based saucepan with the sugar and heat gently to dissolve. Squeeze excess water out of the gelatine and add to the sugar syrup, stirring gently to dissolve. Heat to 90°C, but do not allow to boil. Remove from the heat and add the remaining sauterne. Cool over a bowl of ice. Slowly pour in the champagne. Ladle the jelly into 6 x 100 ml moulds and transfer to the fridge for 4–5 hours to set.

Strawberries
Purée the 6 large strawberries with the caster sugar. Add enough cold water to form a coulis. Cut the remaining strawberries in half and toss in the coulis so they are lightly coated.

Honey Sabayon
Put the egg yolks, sugar, honey and apple juice in a large stainless steel or copper bowl. Whisk over a pan of simmering water until the mixture forms a thick light foam that leaves a ribbon-like trail. It should roughly triple in volume. Cool over a bowl of ice, stirring continuously. When cool, fold in the soft whipped cream. Keep at room temperature until ready to serve (the sabayon can be made up to half an hour ahead of time).

To Serve
Chill 6 dessert plates. Unmould the jellies onto the centre of each plate. Arrange a mound of strawberries next to each jelly and drizzle over the sabayon. Serve straight away.

Serves 6

The rich complex characters of a botrytis affected Semillon (Sauterne) will provide an interesting counterpoint to the sauterne jelly as well as the sweet figs and honey.

Bitter Chocolate Mousse with Lemon–Coriander Sorbet

Frank Fol

Bitter Chocolate Mousse
500 g best quality dark Belgian chocolate
100 g unsalted butter
1 tablespoon cocoa powder
10 egg yolks
4 egg whites
100 g caster sugar, plus 2 tablespoons
400 ml pure cream

Lemon-Coriander Sorbet
300 g sugar
150 ml water
3 sprigs fresh coriander, chopped to a rough paste, plus 10 extra leaves
250 ml lemon juice
peel of 3 lemons

Yellow Syrup
100 g caster sugar
100 ml water
50 g sweetcorn, puréed

Bitter Chocolate Mousse
Break the chocolate into chunks and put in a large bowl with the butter and cocoa powder. Stand over a pan of simmering water and stir occasionally until melted and smooth. Remove from the heat and leave to cool to room temperature. Stir in the egg yolks. Whisk the egg whites with 2 tablespoons caster sugar until they form stiffish peaks. Fold the egg whites into the chocolate mixture. Whip the cream with 100 g sugar until it forms soft floppy peaks and fold into the mousse mixture. Chill until lightly firm.

Lemon-Coriander Sorbet
Put the sugar and water in a heavy-based pan and heat until the sugar dissolves. Bring to the boil, then lower the heat and simmer for 5 minutes to form a light syrup. Add the coriander paste and leave to infuse as the syrup cools. Pour through a chinois or fine sieve and chill. When ready to freeze, measure 250 ml of the coriander syrup and add it to the lemon juice. Stir in the lemon peel and whole coriander leaves. Pour into an ice cream machine and churn according to the manufacturer's instructions.

Yellow Syrup
Put the sugar and water in a heavy-based saucepan and heat until the sugar dissolves. Bring to the boil, then lower the heat and simmer for 5 minutes to form a light syrup. Stir in the sweetcorn and leave to infuse as the syrup cools. Pour through a chinois or fine sieve and chill.

To Serve
Place a spoonful of mousse in the middle of each dessert plate. Arrange a neat scoop of sorbet next to the mousse and drizzle the plate with the yellow syrup.

Serves 6

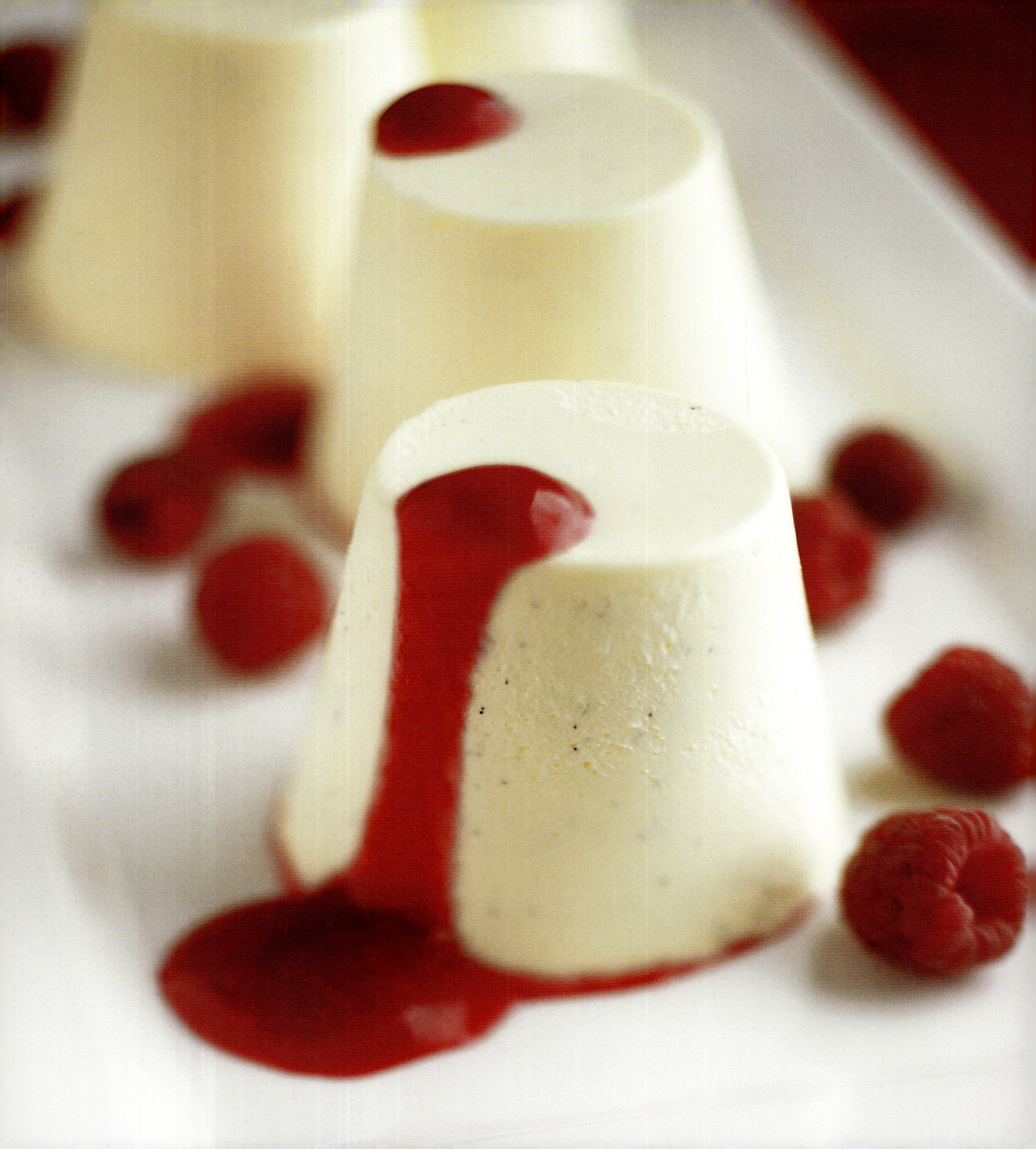

Panna Cotta with Fresh Raspberries and Grappa Jacopo Poli Pinot

Darren Simpson

Use perfect raspberries and the best quality grappa you can lay your hands on.

Panna Cotta
600 ml thickened cream
2 large strips lemon peel, pith removed
1 vanilla bean, split and seeds scraped
1 ¼ leaves of leaf gelatine
　soaked in cold water to soften
75 g caster sugar

Raspberry Sauce
100 g caster sugar
100 ml water
2 punnets raspberries
a squeeze of lemon juice

Garnish
6–8 raspberries per person
grappa Jacopo Poli Pinot Nero
　(or another good quality Italian grappa)

Panna Cotta
Place half the cream in a saucepan with the lemon peel, vanilla pod and seeds. Bring to the boil and cook for 4–5 minutes. Remove from the heat. Squeeze out any excess water from the gelatine and add to the cream, whisking gently until it dissolves. Allow to cool then pour through a fine sieve.

Whisk the remaining cream with the sugar to soft floppy peaks. Fold the two creams together until smooth. Pour into lightly oiled dariole moulds or ramekin dishes and refrigerate overnight until set.

Raspberry Sauce
Put the sugar and water in a heavy-based saucepan and heat slowly until the sugar has dissolved. Bring to the boil, then lower the heat and simmer for about 5 minutes to form a light syrup. Remove from the heat and allow to cool. Place the syrup, raspberries and lemon juice in a blender and purée. Push the sauce through a fine sieve to remove the seeds.

To Serve
Unmould the panna cottas onto each dessert plate. Drizzle each one with the raspberry sauce and a good splash of grappa and garnish with fresh raspberries,

Serves 6–8

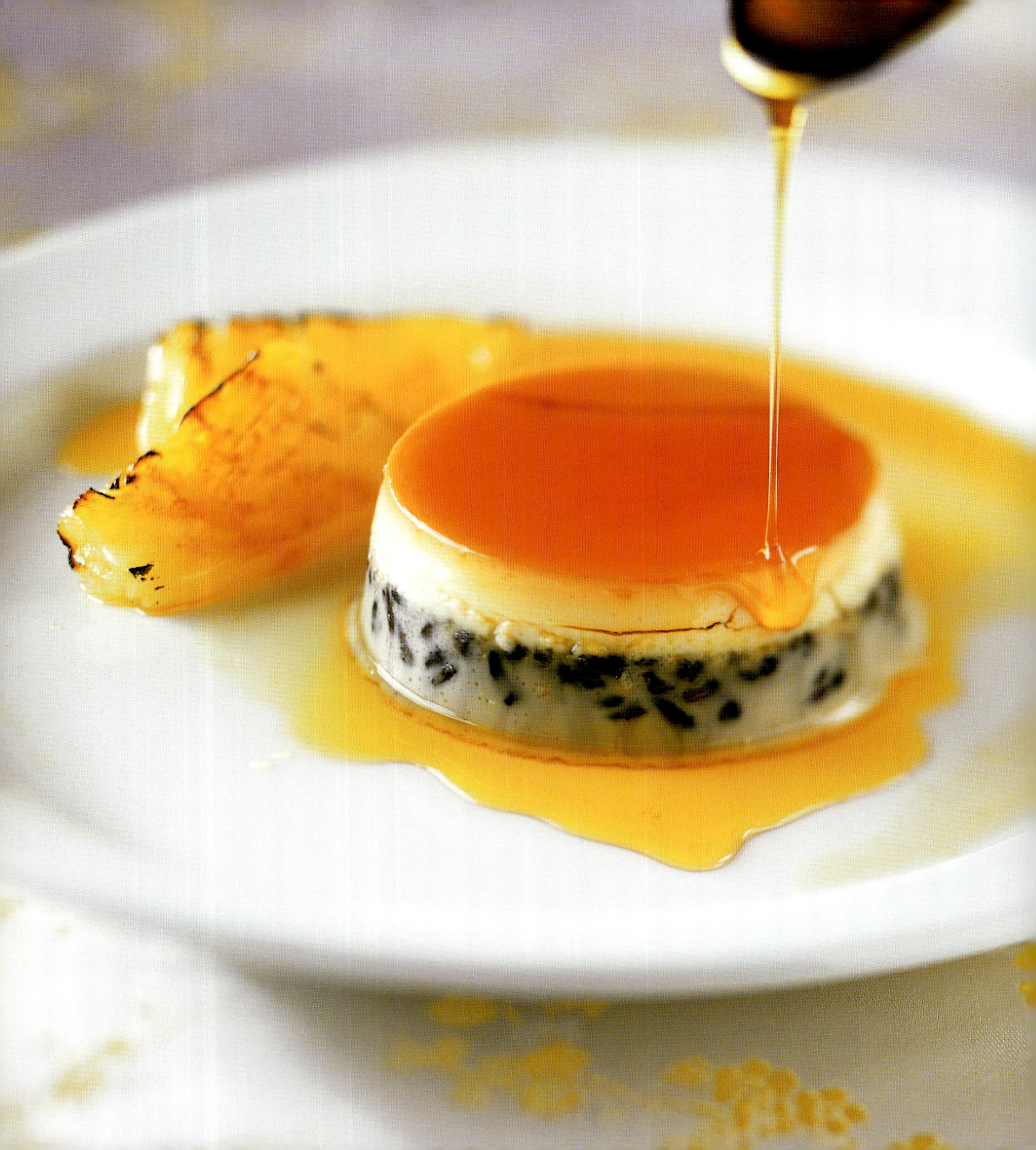

Black Rice and Palm Sugar Pudding with Caramelised Pineapple and Vanilla

Black Rice
75 g black rice
150 ml water
pinch of salt

Caramel Sauce
200 g caster sugar
100 ml water

Custard
500 ml litre milk
100 g desiccated coconut
75 g palm sugar
2 eggs
4 egg yolks

Caramelised Pineapple and Vanilla
500 g caster sugar
500 ml water
1 ripe acid-free pineapple, skin and eyes removed
1 vanilla bean
icing sugar

Black Rice
Place in a heavy-based saucepan with the water and salt. Bring to the boil, then reduce to a simmer and cook until tender (rice splits open).

Caramel Sauce
Mix the water and sugar in a small saucepan and heat until the sugar dissolves. Cook on a medium heat to make a dark caramel. Remove from the heat as soon as it starts to turn brown; it will continue to cook away from the heat. Brush the inside of the pan with water from time to time to stop it crystallising. Clean and lightly oil 6 small dariole moulds. Line with a little caramel and allow to cool. Dilute the remaining caramel with water until it has the consistency of a sauce and set aside until ready to serve.

Custard
Preheat the oven to 150°C. Scald the milk and add the desiccated coconut and palm sugar. Allow to stand and infuse for 30 minutes before straining. Lightly beat together the eggs and egg yolks. Pour on the warm milk and stir well. Pour half the custard mixture into the dariole moulds and cook in a bain-marie in the oven for about about 30 minutes. Just before the custards are completely set, remove from the oven and spoon in a layer of black rice. Top with more custard mixture and return to the oven for a further 10 minutes, or until the custards are set. Remove from the oven and allow to cool. Chill in the fridge.

Caramelised Pineapple and Vanilla
Place the water and sugar in a saucepan and stir over a high heat until dissolved. Bring to the boil, then remove from the heat and allow to cool. Cut the pineapple into 6 rings and remove the hard inner core. Poach in the sugar syrup with the vanilla bean until tender – about 15 minutes. Remove the pineapple slices from the syrup and set aside until ready to serve.

To Serve
Preheat your grill to its highest temperature. Cut each pineapple ring into chunks, sprinkle with icing sugar and place under the grill until caramelised.

Carefully unmould the rice puddings onto each plate, drizzle over a little caramel sauce and serve with the grilled pineapple.

Serves 6

Cheong Liew

It gives me enormous satisfaction to see people enjoying themselves and hearing the story that the food tells them about their own great country: of the wonderful diversity of produce we enjoy and of the contribution made by all its people. I believe that food and wine in Australia have truly come of age!

Malaysian-born Cheong Liew is consultant chef to the Grange Restaurant at the Adelaide Hilton. In 1999 he was awarded an Order of Australia Medal for his services to food, and for 'developing and influencing the style of contemporary Australian cuisine'. Cheong is a great teacher, a writer and a food ambassador for South Australia. He creates dishes that seamlessly blend the east and west and demonstrate the breadth of his imagination and the extraordinary depth of his knowledge.

It's harvest time and the Hunter Valley is a hive of activity. The grapes are picked and pressed and excitement grows about the new vintage. As the days start to shorten the fields are ablaze with autumnal colours. In the kitchen we preserve earth's bounty for the cold months ahead.

autumn

Cauliflower and Cheddar Soup with Gruyère Parcels and Chive Oil

Ralph Potter

Cauliflower and Cheddar Soup
150 g butter
75 g leek, white part only, sliced
75 g onion, sliced
500 g cauliflower
750 g sebago potatoes, peeled and diced
1.75 litres water
1 tablespoon salt
200 mature cheddar cheese, grated

Chive Oil
1 bunch chives
200 ml olive oil

Gruyère Parcels
12 wonton wrappers
100 g gruyère cheese, grated
vegetable oil for deep frying

Cauliflower and Cheddar Soup
Melt the butter in a heavy-based saucepan, add the leeks and onions and sweat gently until they soften. Cut the cauliflower into small florets and add to the pan with the potatoes. Stir well and add the water and salt. Simmer for about an hour. Use a hand blender to purée the soup while it is still warm. Add the cheese and purée again until the cheese has melted and the soup is smooth. Keep until ready to serve.

Chive Oil
Put the chives in a food processor with the olive oil and blend to a purée. Strain the mixture through a fine sieve into a clean jar or squeezy bottle. Keep until ready to use.

Gruyère Parcels
Lay 12 wonton wrappers out on a clean work surface. Wet the edges with a little water and place a small ball of grated cheese in the centre of each. Fold over the corners to form triangles and seal the edges, taking care to exclude any air.

To Serve
Heat the vegetable oil in a wok or saucepan and deep-fry the cheese parcels, a few at a time, until crisp and golden. Remove from the oil and drain on absorbent paper. Gently reheat the soup, taking care not to let it boil, or it will go grainy.

Ladle the soup in shallow bowls, and drizzle with a little chive oil. Top each bowl with two gruyère parcels and serve straight away.

Serves 6

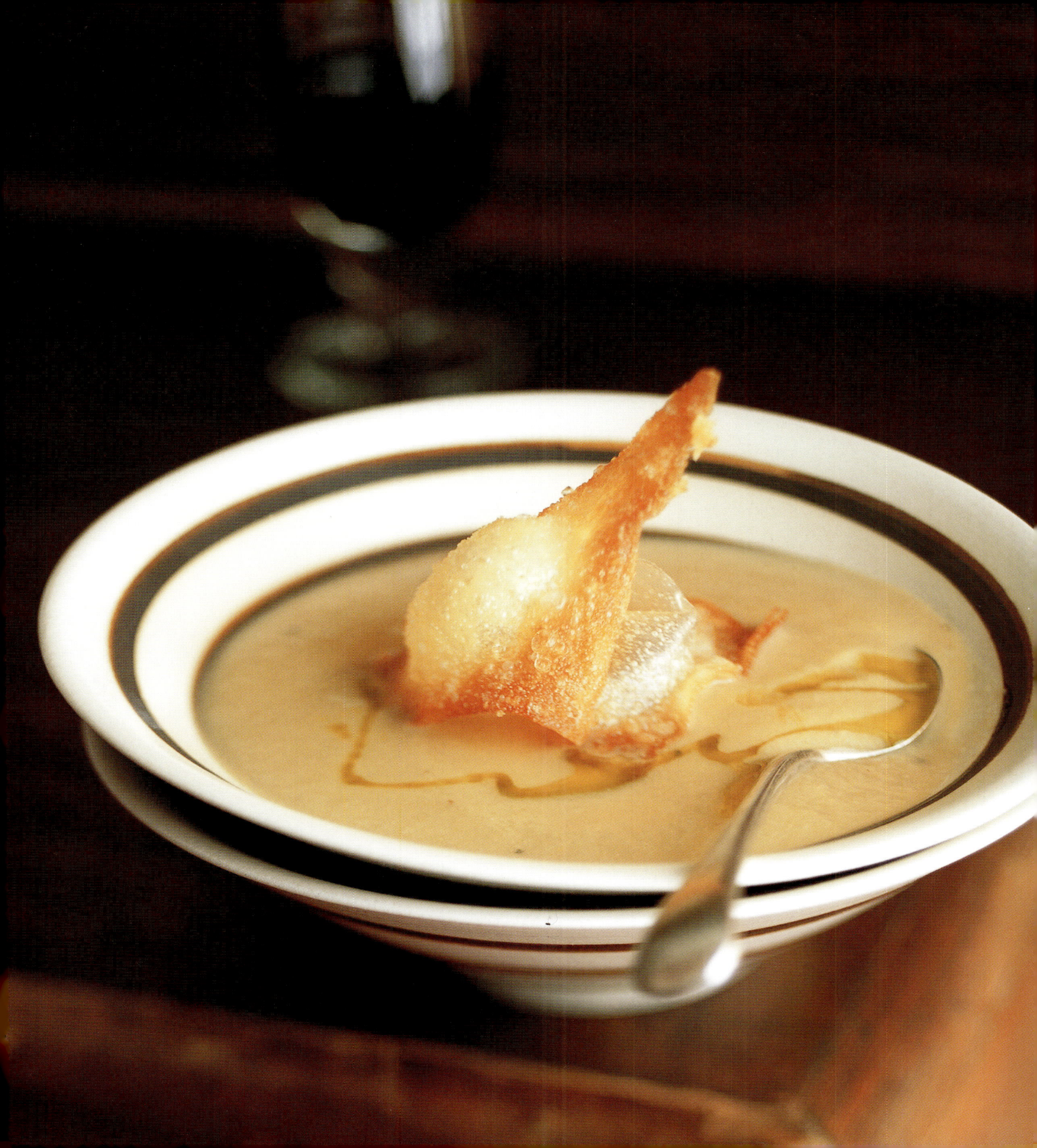

Dietmar Sawyere

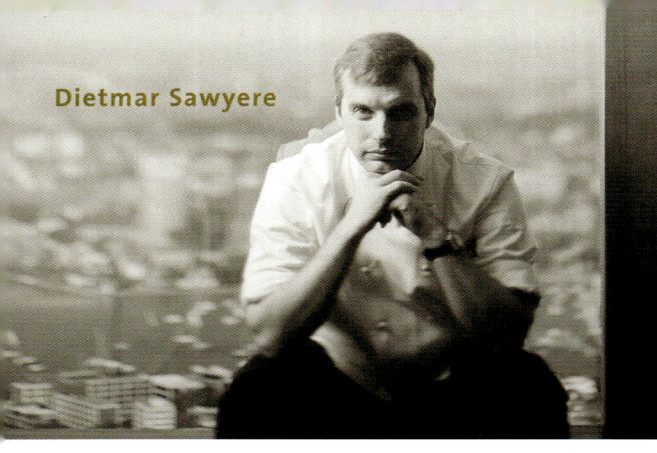

I want our guests to remember their dining experiences, whether at the restaurant or in a vineyard. If they don't, then we have failed!

Swiss-born Dietmar Sawyere began his cooking career in the kitchens of London's prestigious Savoy and Connaught Hotels. He has been operating the glamorous restaurant Forty One in Sydney since 1992, winning more than 40 restaurant and food awards. Dietmar is in constant demand for guest chef appearances, at home and abroad. He consults to Singapore Airlines and operates a second fine-dining restaurant, Five City Road, in Auckland, New Zealand.

Tartare of Tuna and Salmon with Beetroot Oil

300 g yellowfin tuna, cut into 5 mm dice
300 g Atlantic salmon, cut into 5 mm dice
juice of 1/2 lemon
2 tablespoons good quality mayonnaise
1 tablespoon crème fraîche or sour cream
sea salt and freshly ground white pepper
60 g salmon roe
1/2 bunch chives, finely chopped
1/2 bunch chervil, picked into sprigs
6 slices of sourdough toast

Beetroot Oil
3 large beetroot
1 tablespoon lemon juice
1 tablespoon grapeseed oil

Beetroot Oil
Wash the beetroots and put them through a juicer. Pour the beetroot juice into a non-reactive saucepan and add the lemon juice. Bring to the boil then lower the heat and simmer until the juice is reduced by half. Strain through a fine sieve into a clean pan and return to the boil. Simmer again until the juice reaches a syrup consistency. Remove from the heat and whisk in the grapeseed oil. Reserve until ready to use.

To Serve
Put the diced tuna and salmon into a large mixing bowl. Add the lemon juice, mayonnaise and crème fraîche and season lightly. Mix to combine. Divide the tartare between 6 plates, spooning it into nice neat mounds in the centre of each plate. Top with a little salmon roe and sprinkle with the chopped herbs. Drizzle a little beetroot oil around the plate and serve straight away with sourdough toast.

Serves 6

Try a light spicy Pinot Noir that will not dominate the subtle flavours of the raw fish in this light starter.

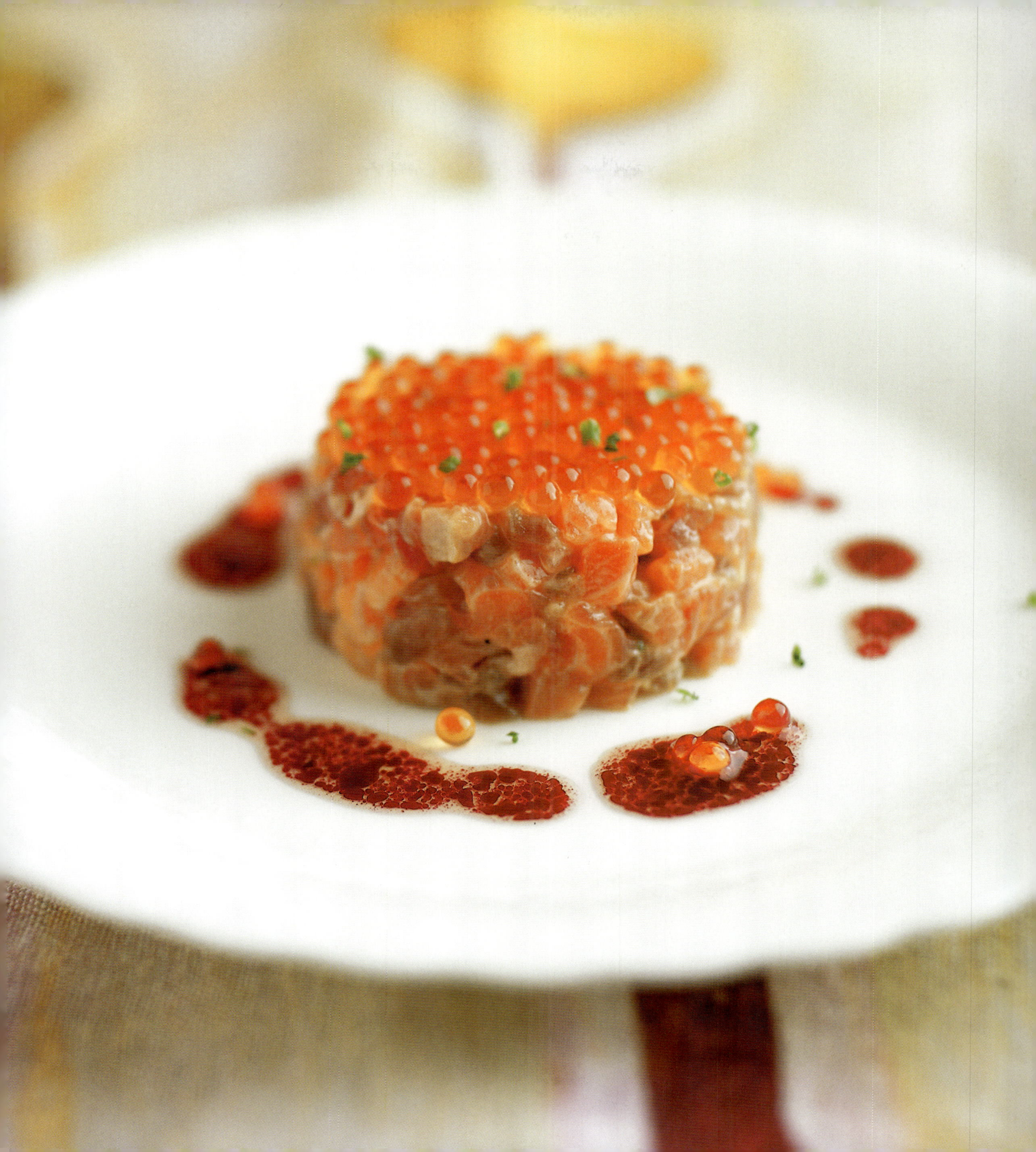

Marinated Olives, Semi-Dried Tomatoes and Brandade de Morue

Tony Bilson

The tomatoes are best dried in an oven with a convection fan.

Marinated Olives
1 kg small Provencale olives
olive oil
3 thin slices of lemon
6 cloves garlic, smashed
3 sprigs thyme
3 sprigs rosemary
2 bay leaves

Semi-dried Tomatoes
2 kg egg-shaped tomatoes
caster sugar
salt
garlic cloves, cut into slivers
fresh thyme broken into small sprigs

Brandade de Morue
1 kg salted cod (also called baccalau)
450 g potatoes, peeled
200 ml milk, warm
300 ml olive oil, warm
pepper

Marinated Olives
Put the olives in a deep jar or plastic container and pour on enough olive oil to cover completely. Add the lemon slices, garlic cloves and herbs and leave to marinate for a week.

Semi-dried Tomatoes
Bring a large pan of water to the boil. Score each tomato with a small cross at each end. Immerse the tomatoes in the boiling water for about 10 seconds to loosen their skins then refresh them under cold water. Slip off the skins and cut the tomatoes into quarters lengthwise. Squeeze out the seeds and pat them dry with absorbent paper.

Preheat the oven to its lowest level (around 35°C) with the fan on. Line a couple of baking trays with silicone paper and arrange the tomato quarters in rows. Sprinkle the tomatoes with sugar and a little salt. On top of each tomato quarter arrange a sliver of garlic and a sprig of thyme. Put the tomatoes in the oven and leave until they dry to the consistency of moist dried apricots. Once ready, remove from the oven and leave to cool. The tomatoes can be stored as they are in the refrigerator or covered with oil and stored in a screw-top jar.

Brandade de Morue
Soak the cod in cold water for 24 hours, changing the water twice during this time. Drain the cod and place it in a saucepan with fresh water. Bring to the boil, then lower the heat and simmer for 10 minutes, or until tender. Remove from the heat and drain off the water. Remove the bones. Meanwhile, cook the potatoes until tender then drain well. Put the hot cod and potatoes into an electric mixer. Mix slowly until the cod and potato begin to coagulate. Add the warm milk and continue mixing until it is absorbed. Slowly pour in the warm olive oil in a steady thin stream, as if making a mayonnaise. Season with pepper, tip into a container and refrigerate until ready to serve.

Serve the olives, semi-dried tomatoes and brandade as an appetiser with plenty of crusty bread or grissini.

Serves 6

The lime and lemon fruit flavours of a medium-bodied Riesling will perfectly complement the savoury flavours in this antipasto-style starter.

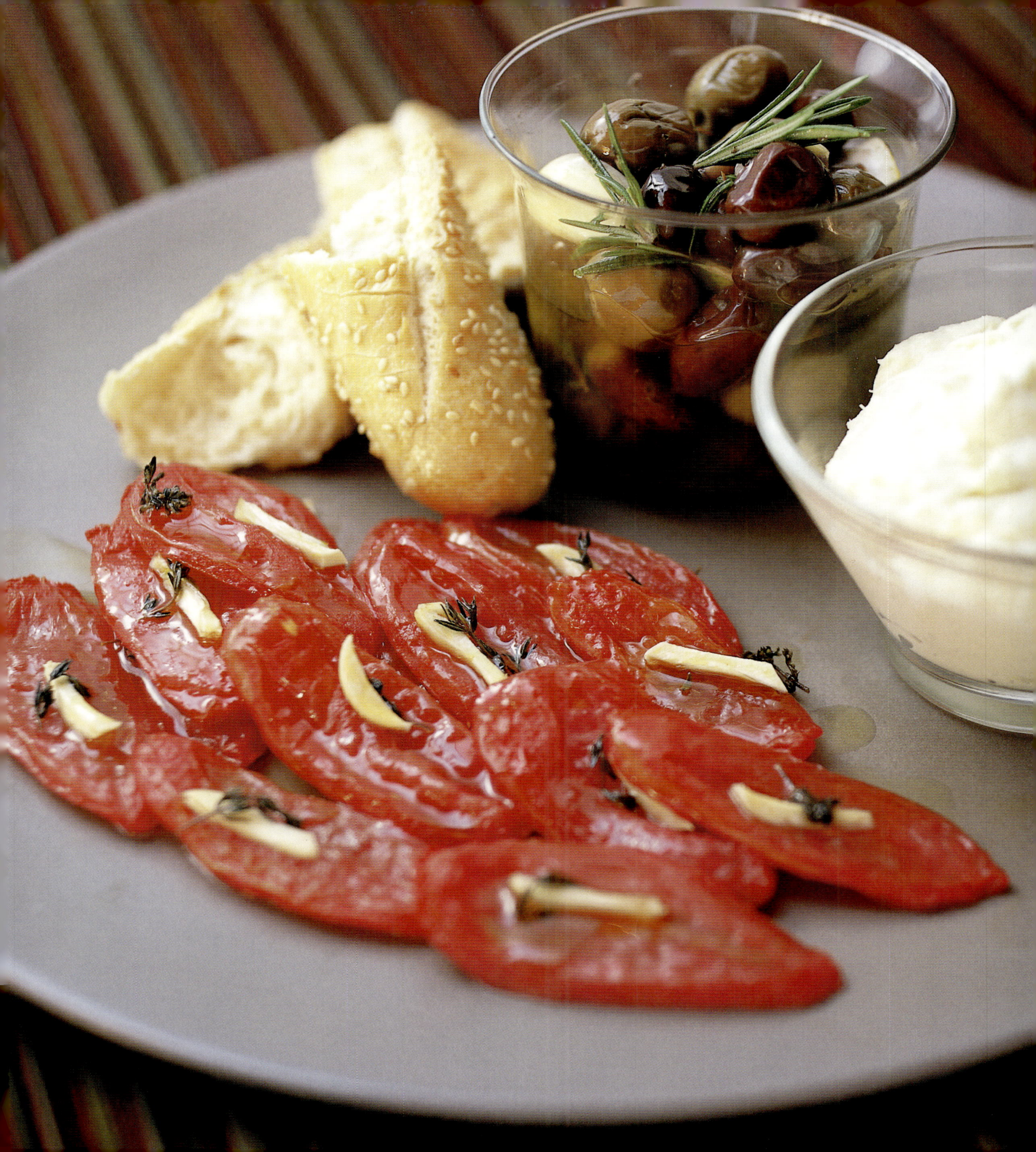

Rotolo of Smoked Salmon, Lime Mascarpone and Salsa Verde

Marc Polese, restaurateur
Brett Deverall, chef

18 slices smoked salmon

Lime Mascarpone
500 g mascarpone
70 ml lime juice
1 bunch dill, stalks removed

Salsa Verde
½ loaf of Italian ciabatta bread, crust removed
150 ml red wine vinegar
4 packed cups parsley leaves
150 g capers, roughly chopped
150 g gherkins, roughly chopped
2 cloves garlic, roughly chopped
4 anchovy fillets
1 hard-boiled egg
100 ml olive oil
juice of 1 lemon

Pasta
6 whole eggs
200 g cooked silverbeet, puréed
juice of 1 lemon
1 kg plain flour
salt and pepper

Lime Mascarpone
Mix the ingredients together and refrigerate overnight to set firm.

Salsa Verde
Roughly chop the ciabatta bread into cubes and soak in the red wine vinegar for a few minutes. Squeeze dry, reserving the vinegar, and put bread into a food processor. Add the parsley, capers, gherkins, garlic, anchovy and egg and pulse until the ingredients form a coarse purée. With the motor running, add the olive oil, lemon juice and the red wine vinegar. Blend briefly until incorporated.

Pasta
Put the eggs and the silverbeet into an electric mixer and add the lemon juice. Attach the dough hook and mix to incorporate. With the motor running slowly, gradually add the flour until all is incorporated and season to taste. When the mixture has formed a smooth dough, turn it out onto a clean work surface and knead briefly into a smooth ball. Wrap in cling film and leave to rest overnight in the fridge.

Use a pasta machine or hand roll the dough into 6 long thin sheets, about 35 cm x 15 cm.

Cook the pasta sheets in boiling water then dry them on a clean tea towel. Lay 6 large sheets of aluminium foil out on your work surface and lay a sheet of pasta dough on top of each. Use a spatula to spread each pasta sheet evenly with the lime mascarpone. Divide the smoked salmon slices between the 6 pasta sheets and lay them out on top of the mascarpone. Smear over a thin layer of salsa verde. Carefully roll up each pasta sheet, using the foil to help you. When rolled, twist both ends of the foil tightly. Refrigerate for 6 hours so the rotolo set firm.

To Serve
Unwrap each rotolo from the foil and slice into medallions. Arrange the medallions on each plate and serve garnished with a salad made with finely sliced fennel and baby rocket leaves, tossed with a little extra-virgin olive oil and lemon juice.

Serves 6

Buffalo Ricotta Tart with Tomatoes, Pesto and Caperberries

Ben Moechtar, sommelier
Mark Stone, chef

250 g buffalo milk ricotta
2 eggs
130 g double cream
50 g flour
1 clove garlic, chopped
zest of 1 lemon
1 teaspoon salt
200 g dried breadcrumbs
80 g butter, melted
1 jar (150 g) chunky tomato relish

Garnish
350 g pesto
300 ml fresh tomato sauce
caperberries

Preheat the oven to 175°C. Put the ricotta in a large mixing bowl and stir until smooth and creamy. Add the eggs one at a time, beating in well. Stir in the cream. Mix together the flour, garlic, lemon zest and salt and add to the cheese mixture, stirring until well combined.

Prepare 6 small ring moulds (about 5 cm deep) or one 20 cm spring-form tin. Grease the moulds well and line their bases with baking parchment. Cut a strip of baking parchment about twice the height of the moulds (to allow for the filling rising in the oven) and grease and line the inside of each mould. Mix the melted butter into the breadcrumbs and pack it down gently in the moulds to form the base. Spread over a layer of chunky tomato relish, then pipe or spoon in enough cheese mixture to fill the moulds two-thirds of the way up. Bake for 20 minutes, or until firm to the touch (it may take longer if you use one large tin).

To Serve
Carefully remove the tarts from the moulds. Serve warm with a dollop of pesto and fresh tomato sauce. Garnish each tart with a few caperberries and scatter some more around the plate.

Serves 6

The soft cherry and strawberry fruit flavours of a pinot noir will soften the crisp, sharp components of this tart. At the same time, the intrinsic dryness of the wine will complement the rich creaminess of the ricotta cheese. Pinot noir wines tend to be quite subtle, so won't compete with the strong, salty flavours of both the caperberries and the pesto in this dish.

Derek Davis

I love the change of the seasons; it allows us to make new friends and renew old relationships. I especially love autumn. We have enjoyed summer's bounty - but enough tomatoes and basil already!

Philadelphia born and bred, Derek Davis has been fascinated with food since he was nine years old. His formal training took place in some of America's great restaurant kitchens (Le Cirque, Le Bernadin, the Rattlesnake Club, Watergate). Today Derek Davis is a chef and entrepreneur. His gastronomic empire includes some of the hottest restaurants in the trendy Manayunk district of Philadelphia (Sonoma, Kansas City Prime, Carmella's, Main Street Bakery). Derek is widely acknowledged as spearheading the development of the area with his accessible and popular 'Italifornia' cuisine.

Grilled Prawns Three Ways

All three types of marinade can be made up to 2 days ahead of time. The longer the prawns marinate, the better the flavour!

18 king prawns
1 large corn muffin, or 2 slices corn bead
6 cups rocket leaves
butter
500 g soft creamy goat's cheese

Raspberry Marinade and Salad Vinaigrette
500 g raspberries
2 shallots, peeled and roughly chopped
2 teaspoons honey
1 tablespoon raspberry vinegar
salt and pepper
2 tablespoons extra-virgin olive oil

Green Tomato Marinade and Salsa
6 large green tomatoes, chopped
2 small cloves garlic, chopped
1 small shallot, peeled and chopped
1 teaspoon chopped coriander
1 small red serrano chilli, minced
salt and pepper

Saffron Marinade
Juice of 1 lemon
pinch of saffron threads
1 clove garlic
1 teaspoon thyme leaves, chopped
1 tablespoon extra-virgin olive oil
1 teaspoon chopped parsley

Raspberry Marinade and Salad Vinaigrette
Put half the raspberries in a food processor with the shallots, honey and vinegar. Pulse until smooth and season with salt and pepper. Tip half of the purée into a mixing bowl and toss 6 of the prawns until well coated. Set aside to marinate.

To make the vinaigrette, add the extra-virgin olive oil to the remaining purée and mix well. Reserve the remaining raspberries for the salad garnish.

Green Tomato Marinade and Salsa
Mix all the ingredients together well. Taste and adjust seasoning. Place half the mixture in a blender and blend to a smooth purée. Tip this purée into a mixing bowl and toss 6 of the prawns until well coated. Set aside to marinate. Reserve the remaining salsa.

Saffron Marinade
Put the lemon juice into a small bowl and add the saffron. Leave to steep for 5 minutes to extract the bright yellow colour. Add the remaining ingredients, stir to combine and leave for a further 5 minutes. Toss the final 6 prawns until well coated and set aside to marinate.

To Serve
Preheat the grill or barbecue. Tear the corn muffin (or bread) into pieces, butter and toast under grill or on barbecue. Thread one of each of the prawns onto skewers (one skewer per person) and grill for a couple of minutes on each side, until the prawns are cooked through. Toss the rocket leaves with the raspberry vinaigrette and divide between 6 plates. Sprinkle over the crumbled cheese and top the salad with a few pieces of toasted corn muffin. Arrange the prawn skewers on top of the salad, and garnish with the fresh raspberries and a dollop of green tomato salsa.

Serves 6

Choose a crisp, fruity Riesling to balance the richness of the prawns.

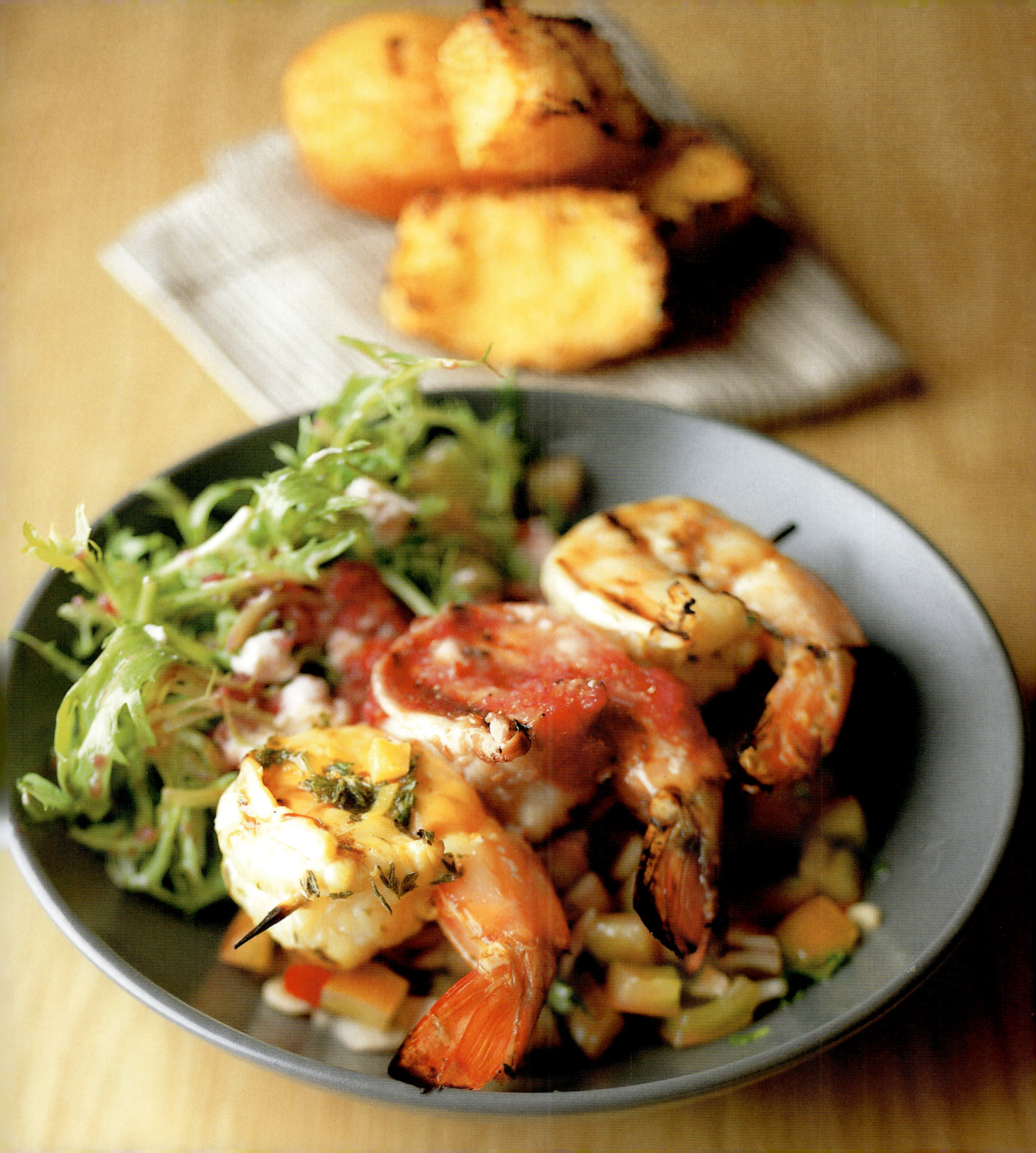

Yellow Chicken Curry with Banana, Pineapple, Onion and Coriander in Coconut Cream

Greg George

6 chicken thigh fillets
20 ml oil
2 onions, diced
300 g fresh pineapple wedges
4 teaspoons yellow curry paste
2 x 400 ml cans coconut cream
30 g sugar
2 tablespoons fish sauce
10 fresh kaffir lime leaves
3 bananas, diced
sprigs of coriander

Cut chicken into chunky dice. Heat oil in a heavy-based pan and sauté chicken until lightly browned. Remove from pan and sauté onion until it is soft. Return chicken to pan, add pineapple and curry paste and cook for a couple of minutes. Pour in coconut cream. Dissolve sugar in fish sauce and add, along with kaffir lime leaves. Bring to the boil and reduce heat to simmer until chicken is cooked – about 25–30 minutes. When almost ready, add diced banana.

Serve
Put a portion of chicken curry on individual plates and garnish with coriander sprigs. Serve with steamed Jasmine rice and tomato relish as an accompaniment.

Serves 6

The fresh, crisp palate of a minerally Riesling will complement the richness of the curry, soften the tannic quality of banana and not interfere with the fruit flavours in this dish.

Fennel-Crusted Guinea Fowl with Rosemary and Figs

Marc Polese, restaurateur
Brett Deverall, chef

6 x guinea fowl supremes (breast with wing bone attached, skin on)
6 x guinea fowl legs
100 ml extra-virgin olive oil
1 large sprig of rosemary, leaves only, roughly chopped
100 ml white wine
30 g cold butter, cubed
9 fresh figs
6 tablespoons balsamic vinegar

Fennel Crust
2 tablespoons fennel seeds
1 1/2 tablespoons black peppercorns
1/2 tablespoon sea salt
1 tablespoon whole fennel seeds

Fennel Crust
Put 2 tablespoons of fennel seeds and the black peppercorns into a spice grinder or mortar and pestle and grind to a fine powder. Mix with the sea salt and the whole fennel seeds.

Preheat the oven to 180°C. To prepare the guinea fowl, use a sharp knife to make deep cuts in the fleshy part of the guinea fowl legs, right through to the bone (this will help them cook more quickly). Sprinkle the legs and breasts all over with the fennel crust, patting it on lightly.

Heat 50 ml of the olive oil in a large frying pan and sear all the portions of guinea fowl, legs and breasts, until nicely browned all over. This should take about 3–4 minutes for each side. Transfer the guinea fowl to a preheated baking tray and cook for 8–10 minutes. Remove from the oven and allow to rest in a warm place until ready to serve.

Meanwhile, add the chopped rosemary to the oil that is left in the hot frying pan and cook over a medium heat for a minute, stirring constantly to stop it burning. Add the white wine and simmer until it has reduced by one-third. Lower the heat and add the cold butter, whisking gently until it has all melted. Remove from the heat and set aside until ready to serve.

When ready to serve, heat a griddle or frying pan until very hot. Cut the figs in half. Add about 30 ml of the extra-virgin olive oil to the pan and cook the figs, cut side down, until lightly caramelised. Remove from the pan and arrange 3 halves around the edge of each plate.

To Serve
Place a guinea fowl leg in the centre of each plate. Cut each breast in half and lean against the leg. Pour a little of the warm sauce over the guinea fowl. Drizzle the remaining extra-virgin olive oil and a little balsamic vinegar over the figs and serve.

Serves 6

Pinot Noir will provide light fruit and savoury flavours to enhance the complex and subtle flavours of the guinea fowl. It will also be robust enough to stand up to the herbs in this dish.

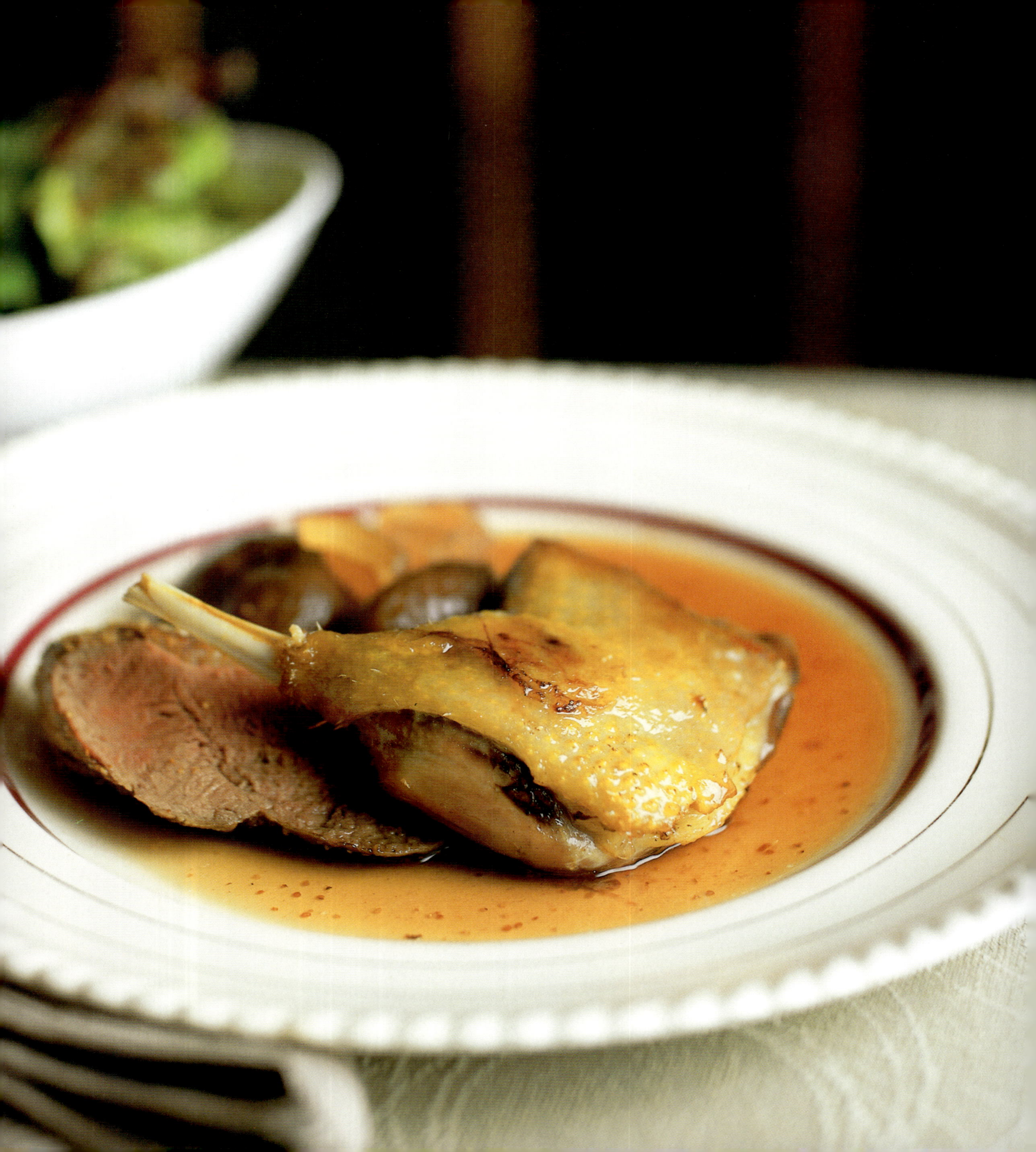

Slow-Roasted Duck with Steamed Figs, Star Anise and Mustard Fruits

Ross Lusted

The duck is prepared in stages. Start 2 days ahead of time to confit the legs and thighs. The duck breasts and figs need to be prepared a day ahead.

Slow-Roasted Duck
2 x 2.3 kg free-range muscovy duck
1 ½ tablespoons sea salt
2 whole star anise, crushed
1 cinnamon stick, crushed
6 black peppercorns, crushed
400 ml duck fat
20 ml olive oil
20 g butter
50 g polenta
1 piece cassia bark,
    broken roughly into large pieces

Steamed Figs, Star Anise and Mustard Fruits
100 g caster sugar
2 whole star anise
500 ml good quality red wine vinegar
6 teaspoons finely chopped mustard fruits
6 ripe figs

Day 1. First, prepare the ducks. Remove the legs and thighs from the ducks, keeping them together. Trim the wing bones and cut away the excess carcass, leaving the breasts still attached to the bone.

Mix the salt with the star anise, cinnamon and peppercorns. Rub into the duck legs and thighs and refrigerate overnight.

Day 2. Preheat the oven to 160°C. Rinse the spice mix off the duck legs and thighs and pat dry. Arrange in an ovenproof dish and pour on the duck fat, ensuring they are completely covered. Cook for 2 ½ hours. Remove from the oven and allow to cool in the duck fat. Refrigerate overnight.

Lower the oven temperature to 60°C. Place the duck breasts, still attached to the carcass, in the oven for an hour. This is important as it 'sets' the protein in the meat without cooking it. Remove from the oven and cool. Refrigerate overnight.

Prepare the figs: put the caster sugar, star anise and vinegar into a large heavy-based pan. Bring to the boil and reduce to about 200 ml. Then allow to cool.

Lightly oil 6 dariole moulds and place a teaspoon of mustard fruits in the bottom of each, then a fig, with the stalk upward. Spoon a tablespoon of the reduced vinegar over each fig and cover the moulds with cling film. Place in a steamer and steam for 10 minutes, until the figs are soft. Allow to cool. Remove the cling film and stack a clean mould inside each filled one. Weight the moulds down and refrigerate overnight to create firm, pressed figs.

Day 3. About half an hour before you are ready to serve, preheat the oven to 180°C. Remove the legs and thighs from the fat. Separate the legs and thighs and roast for 10 minutes, or until crispy. Remove from the oven and leave to rest in a warm place.

Meanwhile, heat the olive oil and butter in a heavy-based, ovenproof frying pan. Slice the duck breasts away from the bone and press, skin side down, in the polenta. Shake off any excess polenta grains and fry the duck breasts, skin side down, for about 5 minutes, or until golden. Turn the breasts over in the cassia bark then transfer the pan to the oven and cook for 5 minutes. Remove from the oven and leave to rest in a warm place.

Gently reheat the figs in a steamer.

To Serve
Divide the confit leg and thigh meat evenly between 6 plates. Slice the duck breast and arrange over the duck and thigh meat. Serve with the warm fig, a little of the fig juices and a simple green salad.

Serves 6

Loin of Lamb with Braised Lentils and Rosemary Aïoli

Ralph Potter

6 x 200 g lamb loins, trimmed
a little olive oil
salt and pepper

Sherry Reduction
50 ml olive oil
75 g shallots, finely chopped
200 ml medium-dry sherry
   (amontillado style)
750 ml lamb or chicken stock

Braised Lentils
100 ml olive oil
75 g onion, finely chopped
75 g carrot, finely diced
50 g celery or celeriac, finely diced
300 g small green lentils,
   very well rinsed and drained
100 g diced seeded tomatoes
750 ml lamb or chicken stock
salt and pepper

Rosemary Aïoli
500 g sebago potatoes, peeled
3 egg yolks
1 clove garlic, crushed
1 tablespoon finely chopped
   rosemary leaves
250 ml olive oil
salt and pepper

Sherry Reduction
Heat the olive oil in a heavy-based saucepan and sweat the shallots until they soften. Add the sherry and simmer until reduced by half. Add the stock and simmer again until reduced by two-thirds. The reduction should be rich and slightly sticky.

Braised Lentils
Heat the olive oil in a heavy-based saucepan and sweat the onion, carrot and celery until they soften. Add the drained lentils to the pan with the diced tomatoes. Add the stock and simmer gently uncovered for about 50 minutes, or until the lentils are cooked. Season with salt and pepper

Rosemary Aïoli
Boil the potatoes in plenty of salted water. Drain them well and mash by hand until smooth. Tip the mashed potato into a food processor and while still warm, add the egg yolks, garlic and rosemary and blend briefly to incorporate. With the motor running, slowly add the olive oil in a thin, steady stream. As soon as the oil is all incorporated, switch off the motor. Season with salt and pepper and keep warm until ready to serve.

Loin of Lamb
When ready to serve, preheat your grill or barbecue to its highest temperature. Brush the lamb loins with olive oil and season with salt and pepper. Cook the lamb loins for about 5 minutes, turning so they cook evenly. Remove from the heat and leave in a warm place to rest for 5 minutes.

To Serve
Spoon some lentils into the centre of each serving plate (use a slotted spoon to drain off any excess liquid). Slice the lamb loins thinly and arrange on top of the lentils. Top the lamb with a good dollop of rosemary aioli and drizzle the plate with the sherry reduction.

Serves 6

Shiraz has the fullness to balance this rich lamb dish and enough spiciness to provide contrast.

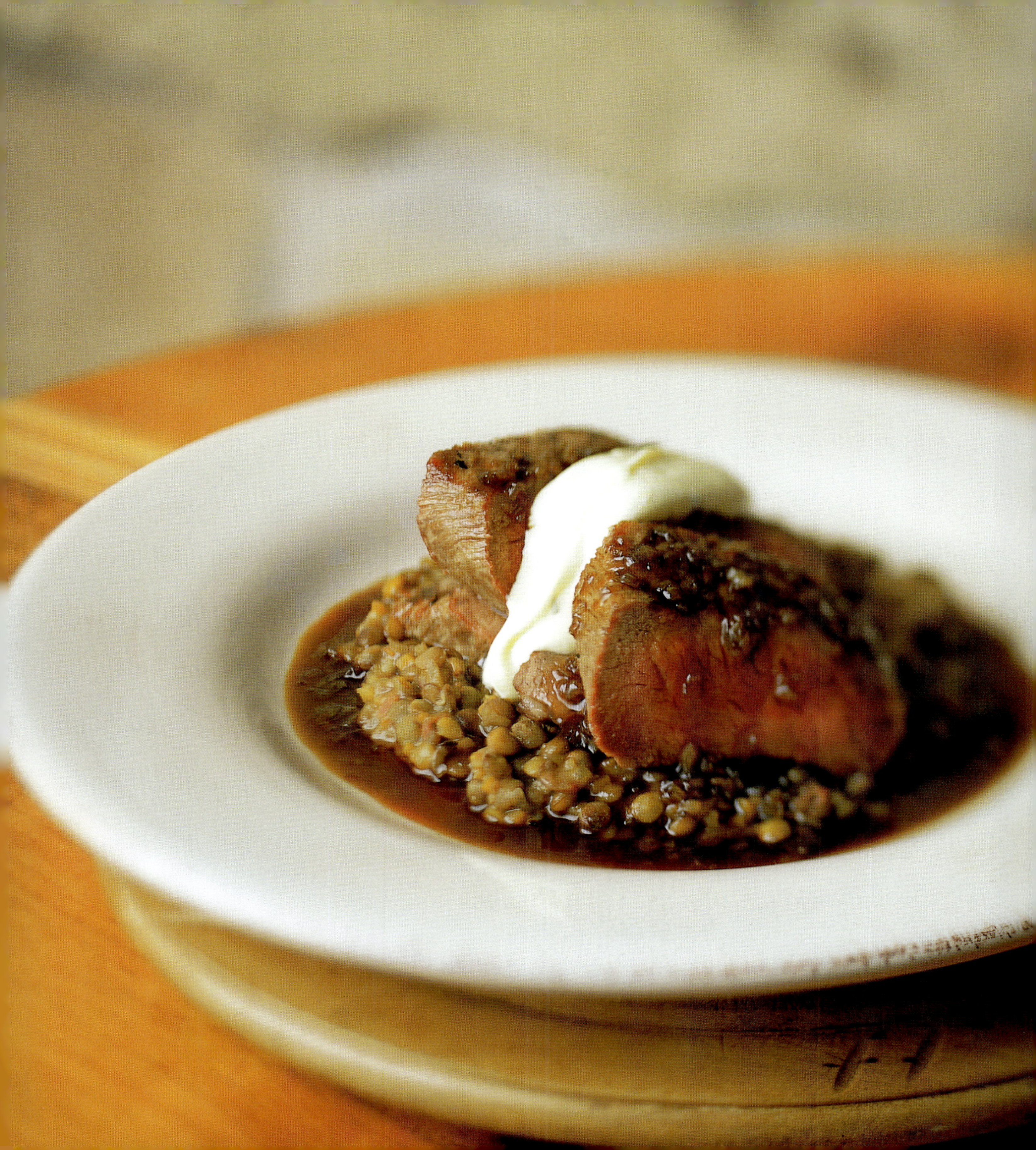

Greg George

The Seasons Plate lunches have given me the amazing experience of cooking with some of the top chefs in Australia. It has been challenging – as every chef has their own style and expectations, but also incredibly rewarding. I learn something new every time!

Greg George is executive chef at Wyndham Estate Winery, where he has been supervising the restaurant and special events for the last ten years. Unlike many other chefs who travel the country to expand their culinary knowledge, Greg is lucky enough to have them come to him! Four times a year he invites some of Australia's leading chefs and food personalities to prepare a menu for the famous Seasons Plate lunch events. Greg estimates that over the years he has developed menus and prepared meals for nearly 20,000 diners as part of the winery's busy calendar.

Seared Hereford Tenderloin Wyndham Estate Style

1 punnet shiitake mushrooms
1 punnet oyster mushrooms
1 punnet button mushrooms
24 asparagus spears, trimmed of woody stems
3 roma tomatoes
50 g butter
50 ml virgin olive oil
salt and freshly ground pepper
6 x 200 g tenderloin beef fillets

Soy, Honey and Chilli Sauce
1.25 litres beef stock
4 tablespoons soy sauce
4 tablespoons Thai sweet chilli sauce
4 tablespoons honey
½ bunch coriander leaves, roughly chopped

Soy, Honey and Chilli Sauce
Put the beef stock in a large saucepan and bring to the boil. Lower the heat and simmer until reduced by about half. Add the soy, chilli sauce and honey. Adjust the seasoning to taste. Remove from the heat and keep until ready to serve. Just before serving, warm the sauce through gently and add the chopped fresh coriander.

To prepare the vegetables, cut all the mushrooms and the roma tomatoes in half. Snap the woody stems off the asparagus. Melt the butter and oil in a heavy-based frying pan and fry the mushrooms until soft then season with salt and freshly ground pepper. Keep warm until ready to serve.

Blanch the asparagus in boiling water until just tender.

Preheat the oven to 140°C. Season the tomatoes with salt and freshly ground pepper. Place them on an oiled baking tray and roast in the oven for 15 minutes. Remove from the oven and keep warm until ready to serve.

When ready to serve, turn the oven temperature up to 180°C. Heat a heavy-based ovenproof frying pan until smoking hot. Rub the beef fillets with olive oil and season with salt and pepper. Sear the beef fillets until they are evenly coloured all over. Transfer the pan to the oven and cook for 15–20 minutes.

To Serve
Divide the mushrooms between 6 plates and top each portion with 4 spears of asparagus. Arrange the beef fillet on top and garnish with the roasted tomato. Drizzle the sauce around the plate and serve straight away.

Serves 6

This 'signature' dish of Wyndham Estate chef, Greg George, is often matched with a full-bodied Cabernet Sauvignon – ideally one with some age to soften the bold fruit flavours and to enhance the sweet spiciness of the sauce.

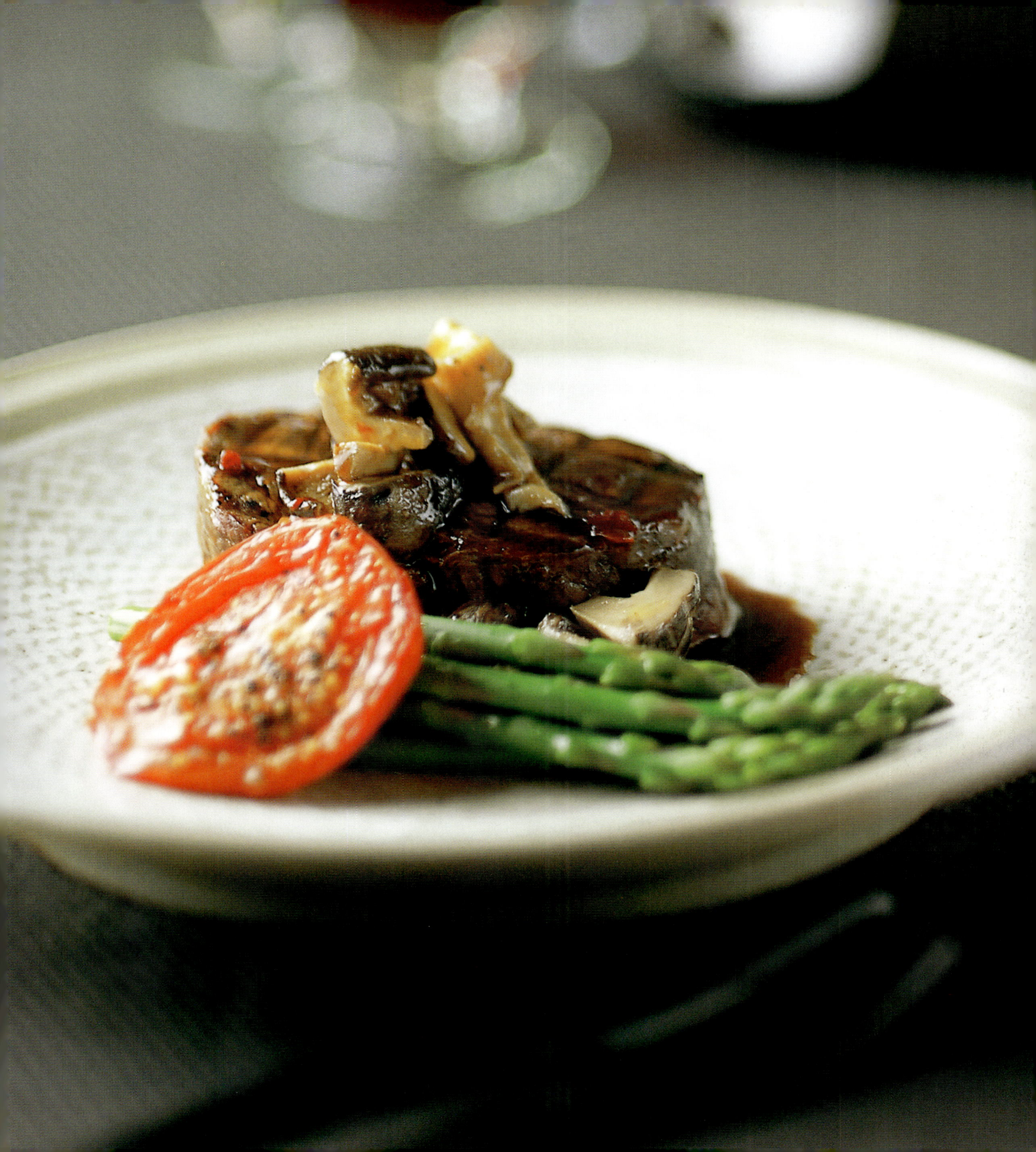

Roast Fillet of Beef with Baby Spinach, Witlof and Madeira Sauce

Dietmar Sawyere

1 x 1.8 kg fillet of beef
100 ml extra-virgin olive oil
1 clove garlic, minced

Garlic Butter
150 g softened butter
4 cloves garlic, minced
squeeze of lemon juice
sea salt and freshly ground white pepper

Baby Spinach and Witlof
75 g butter
100 g sugar
3 heads witlof
400 g baby spinach leaves
50 ml chicken stock

Madeira Sauce
6 shallots, sliced
50 g dried porcini mushrooms
100 g field mushrooms, sliced
50 ml madeira
250 ml chicken stock
1 teaspoon arrowroot (optional)

Garlic Butter
Mix the ingredients together until well combined. Scrape onto a square of cling film and shape into a neat little log. Refrigerate until ready to serve.

Roast Fillet of Beef
In the morning before you wish to serve it, trim the beef fillet and tie it neatly with string in 3 or 4 places along its length. Rub the fillet all over with the oil and garlic, cover and refrigerate. Bring to room temperature before cooking.

Preheat the oven to 200°C. Sear the beef on the stove top until it is evenly coloured all over. Roast in the oven for 25–30 minutes (for medium-rare), turning halfway through the cooking time. Remove from the oven, cover with foil and leave to rest in a warm place for 15 minutes.

Baby Spinach and Witlof
While the beef is cooking, prepare the vegetables. Melt the butter and sugar in a heavy-based saucepan, stirring until the sugar has dissolved. Add the whole witlof and sauté for 2–3 minutes until it begins to soften. Add the chicken stock and continue cooking until the witlof is tender. Remove from the heat and drain the witlof, then cut each one in half. When you are ready to serve, return the witlof to the pan with the spinach leaves and toss together until the spinach is just wilted.

Madeira Sauce
When you are nearly ready to serve, make the madeira sauce. Heat the beef roasting pan and add the shallots, porcini and field mushrooms. Sweat for a few minutes then deglaze the pan with the madeira, stirring well. When it is bubbling, add the chicken stock and simmer for 10 minutes. Strain through a chinois or a fine sieve and return to the stove. Bring back to the boil and thicken with a little arrowroot if desired.

To Serve
Slice the beef fillet into thick slices. Arrange some slices of beef on top of the witlof and spinach and ladle on some madeira jus. Serve with creamy potato purée.

Serves 6

Surf and Turf

Derek Davis

Despite the tongue-in-cheek, retro name, this dish is really terrific. It needs the best quality tuna and beef fillet that you can find.

1 x 700 g piece beef fillet, centre cut
120 ml extra-virgin olive oil
1 teaspoon chopped rosemary leaves
salt and pepper
6 x 120 g yellowfin tuna fillets
½ teaspoon chopped thyme leaves

Whipped Potatoes
500 g potatoes, peeled
3 shallots, peeled and
    roasted until very soft
325 ml cabernet sauvignon
125 ml milk
30 g butter
salt

Red Wine Sauce
125 ml reduced veal stock
325 ml cabernet merlot
2 shallots, peeled and finely chopped
1 small carrot, finely grated
50 g butter
salt and pepper to taste

Grilled Green Vegetables
12 baby leeks, trimmed and blanched
500 g thin green beans,
    trimmed and blanched
40 g butter
salt and pepper

Whipped Potatoes
Boil the potatoes until just cooked through then drain well. Finely chop the roasted shallots and place them in a small saucepan with the cabernet sauvignon. Simmer until the wine has almost completely reduced. Add the milk and butter to the potatoes and whisk in over a low heat until the butter melts. Add the reduced wine mixture to the potatoes and whisk to a smooth purée. Season with salt to taste (do not add pepper as it will overpower the flavour of the potatoes).

Red Wine Sauce
Heat the veal stock in a heavy-based saucepan. Add the wine, shallots and carrot and bring to the boil. Allow to simmer until the sauce has reduced by half. Whisk in the butter then strain the sauce through a fine sieve. Season with salt and pepper to taste. Set aside until ready to serve.

Grilled Green Vegetables
Sear the leeks until they are nicely browned and starting to crisp. Warm the beans through with a little butter. Season the vegetables with a little salt and pepper.

Surf and Turf
To cook the beef fillet, rub it all over with half of the extra-virgin olive oil and the chopped rosemary. Season generously with salt and pepper. Heat a heavy-based frying pan and sear the beef all over so it is nicely coloured. Lower the heat a little and cook for 8–10 minutes, turning constantly. Remove from the pan and leave in a warm place to rest for about 7 minutes.

Rub the tuna with the chopped thyme and season with salt and pepper. Heat the remaining extra-virgin olive oil in the frying pan until smoking hot. Sear the tuna pieces for 40 seconds on each side. Set aside.

To Serve
Place a generous mound of whipped potato on each plate. Top with some steamed green beans. Use a sharp knife and cut the beef into twelve slices. Slice each piece of tuna in half crosswise. Alternate slices of the tuna and beef around the potato. Garnish with the grilled baby leeks. Drizzle the plate with the red wine-butter sauce and serve straight away.

Serves 6

Sauterne and Olive Oil Cake with Roasted Peaches

Ross Lusted

The cake may be made a day ahead of time and gently warmed through in the oven before serving. Store it in an airtight container at room temperature. The roasted peaches may be made a few hours ahead of time, but no earlier or they will become soggy and lose their juices.

Sauterne and Olive Oil Cake
7 eggs
160 g caster sugar
90 ml good quality
   Italian extra-virgin olive oil
100 ml sauterne
150 g plain flour, sifted
40 g icing sugar
120 g mascarpone cheese
   or double cream

Roasted Peaches
200 ml verjuice or
   unsweetened white grape juice
100 g raisins
40 g unsalted butter
3 ripe yellow peaches,
   halved and stone removed
50 g soft brown sugar
100 ml sauterne

Sauterne and Olive Oil Cake
Preheat the oven to 180°C. Separate the eggs and beat 5 of the yolks with half the caster sugar until it turns pale and thickens in volume. (Reserve the remaining 2 yolks for another recipe.) Beat in the olive oil and sauterne. Fold in the sifted flour until well incorporated. Beat the 7 egg whites with the rest of the caster sugar until they form soft peaks. Fold carefully into the egg yolk mixture, taking care not to lose the volume. Pour into a greased loaf tin and bake for 20 minutes. Lower the heat to 150°C and bake for another 20 minutes. Turn off the oven and prop the oven door slightly ajar. Leave the cake in the oven for another 10 minutes, then remove and allow to cool in the tin before turning out. Store at room temperature until ready to serve (do not refrigerate).

Roasted Peaches
To prepare the roasted peaches, place the verjuice in a small pan and heat until nearly boiling. Add the raisins and remove from the heat. Leave to soak for 2 hours, until the raisins have swelled and softened. Strain off the liquor and reserve. Set aside the raisins.

Heat the butter in a large heavy-based frying pan. Add the peaches, cut side down, and fry for about 5 minutes, until golden. Add the sugar and allow to caramelise. Turn the peaches over in the pan and deglaze with the verjuice. Lower the heat to a gentle simmer and poach the peaches gently until the juice has almost completely evaporated. Remove from the heat and reserve at room temperature.

To Serve
Preheat the oven to 180°C. Fill each peach half with a spoonful of raisins. Place in an ovenproof dish and spoon over any remaining juice. Bake for 10 minutes until warmed through.

Dust the cake with icing sugar and cut into slices. Arrange a slice of cake on each plate and serve with a warm peach half and a dollop of mascarpone or double cream.

Serves 6

A sparkling Chardonnay will add freshness to this dessert.

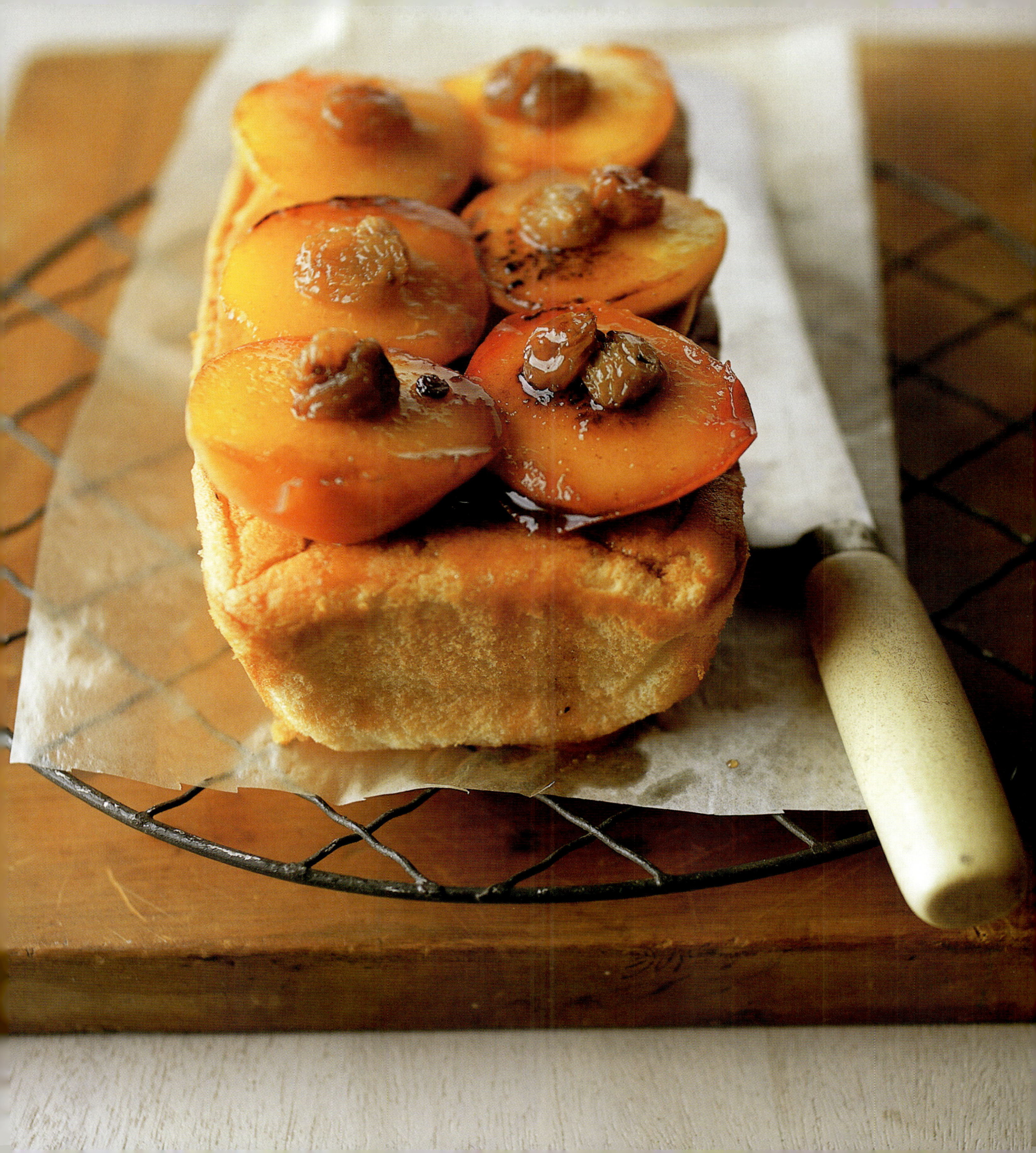

Marmalade, Ginger and Chocolate Pudding

Ralph Potter

250 g dark palm sugar
250 g butter
zest of 8 oranges
50 g finely chopped fresh ginger
5 eggs, roughly beaten
375 g plain flour
25 g baking powder
1 teaspoon orange oil
75 ml orange juice
175 g dark chocolate chips
250 g marmalade
250 g crème fraîche

Use a sharp knife to finely shred the palm sugar then put it into a food processor with the butter, orange zest and chopped ginger. Blend until well combined. Gradually add the beaten egg until it is all incorporated, then tip the mixture out into a large mixing bowl. Sieve the flour and baking powder together and fold into the pudding mixture. Stir in the orange oil and enough of the orange juice to achieve a soft, dropping consistency. Fold in the chocolate chips.

Butter 6 ovenproof moulds and distribute the pudding mixture between them. Cover each pudding with a piece of buttered greaseproof paper and tie in place with string. Place the puddings in a large pan of simmering water covered with a tight-fitting lid or aluminium foil and steam for about 50 minutes, topping up with more boiling water from time to time if needed. The puddings can be prepared to this stage up to a week ahead of time. Store them in the fridge.

To Serve

Gently reheat the puddings in a steamer or in a microwave oven. Unmould puddings and place one in the centre of each dessert plate. Heat the marmalade and pour over the puddings. Serve with a generous spoonful of crème fraîche. The puddings are also delicious with vanilla ice cream.

Serves 6

Choose a lusciously sweet and sticky botrytis-affected Semillon with strong apricot and treacle flavours to match the richness of jam and chocolate in this rich steamed pudding.

Chocolate Fudge Cake with Raspberry Coulis and Double Cream

Greg George

Chocolate Fudge Cake
500 g dark Belgium chocolate
150 g Belgium cocoa powder
250 ml milk
6 eggs
300 g caster sugar
7 egg whites
400 ml cream

Raspberry Coulis
200 g caster sugar
200 ml water
250 g fresh raspberries
double cream to serve

Chocolate Fudge Cake
Preheat the oven to 140°C. Line and grease a 25 cm springform cake tin. Break up the chocolate and place in a large heatproof bowl with the cocoa powder. Stand over a pan of gently simmering water until the chocolate has melted. In a separate pan, bring the milk to the boil. Pour the milk onto the melted chocolate and stir until smooth. Set aside to cool. Put the whole eggs and 200 g of the caster sugar into an electric mixer and beat until the mixture is thick and creamy, then beat in the cooled chocolate mixture.

Whip the egg whites with the remaining 100 g caster sugar until they form stiff peaks and fold into the chocolate mixture. Whip the cream to soft floppy peaks and fold into the mixture. Pour cake batter into the tin and bake for around an hour. The cake will rise during the cooking, but collapse when you take it out of the oven.

Raspberry Coulis
Put the sugar and water into a heavy-based saucepan and heat until the sugar dissolves. Bring to the boil, then lower the heat and simmer for 5 minutes to form a light syrup. Remove the pan from the heat and add the raspberries. Pour the mixture into a blender and blend to a purée. Push the purée through a fine sieve to remove the seeds.

To Serve
Spoon a generous amount of coulis onto the centre of each plate. Arrange a slice of the cake on top of the coulis. Dust with icing sugar and serve with a big dollop of extra-thick double cream.

Serves 6

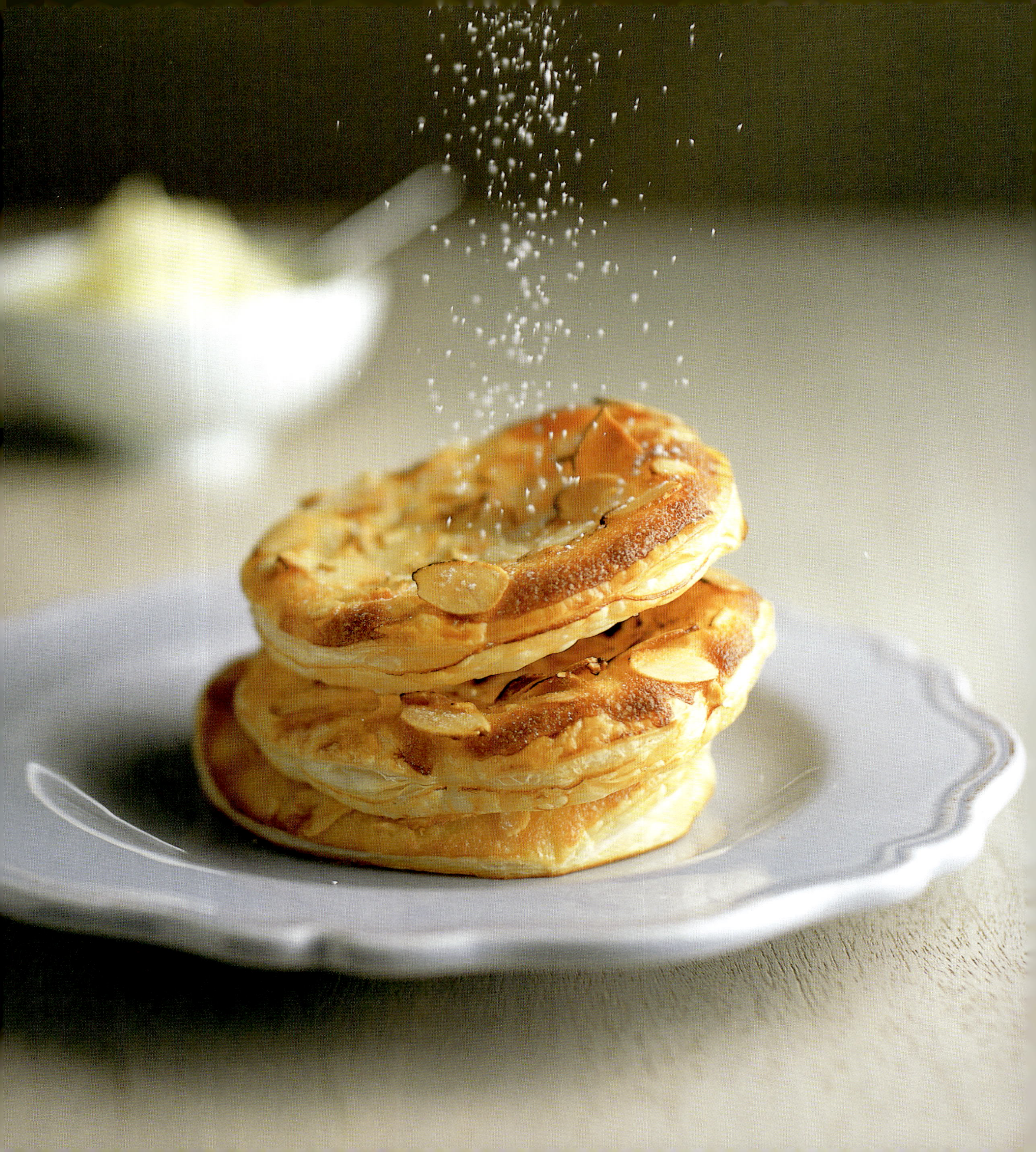

An elder statesman of the Australian food scene, Tony Bilson has dedicated the last three decades of his life to the pursuit of gastronomic excellence. A self-taught chef from Melbourne, Tony has always been a leader in the world of food and wine. His landmark restaurants have included the Berowra Waters Inn, Kinselas, The Treasury and Bilson's, to name but a few. He is a regular contributor to food and wine magazines and the author of five books.

The changes in food and wine in Australia over the last thirty years have added a new dimension to all our lives and enriched our culture.

Tony Bilson

Galette of Almonds with Clotted Cream

Instead of making one large galette, you could also make six small individual galettes, one to serve each person.

Frangipane
150 g softened butter
150 g caster sugar
3 eggs
2 tablespoons Armagnac or brandy
60 g plain flour

500 g butter puff pastry
1 egg yolk
1 tablespoon cream
150 g flaked almonds
icing sugar
clotted cream to serve

Frangipane
Cream the butter and sugar in an electric mixer. Add the eggs and mix until incorporated. Add the Armagnac then fold in the flour.

Preheat the oven to 180°C. Roll the puff pastry out to a circle about 2–3 mm thick and use to line a 25 cm tart tin. Prick the pastry all over with a fork. Mix the egg yolk with the cream to make an egg wash and brush the sides of the tart. Spread the pastry base with the frangipane, leaving the sides free. Sprinkle the flaked almonds evenly over the frangipane. Dust generously with icing sugar. Bake for 10–15 minutes, or until golden brown.

To Serve
Cut the galette into slices and serve warm with clotted cream.

Serves 6

This delicate almond-flavoured dessert will be perfectly matched with a rich, complex botrytis-affected Semillon.

Passionfruit Brulée with Coconut Dacquoise

David Rayner

Prepare the coconut dacquoise and the passionfruit curd the day before you plan to serve this dessert.

Coconut Dacquoise
330 g egg whites (about 11 egg whites)
110 g caster sugar
90 g ground almonds
250 g icing sugar
100 g shredded coconut
125 g desiccated coconut

Passionfruit Curd
750 ml passionfruit juice
1.6 litres pure cream
275 g egg yolks (around 9 egg yolks)
275 g caster sugar
9 x 3 g sheets of gelatine,
   soaked in water and squeezed out
90 g extra caster sugar

Passionfruit Sauce
500 ml passionfruit pulp
500 ml water
500 g caster sugar

Coconut Dacquoise
Preheat the oven to 200°C. Whisk the egg whites until firm peaks form then gradually whisk in the sugar. Mix together the remaining dry ingredients then carefully fold into the egg whites until evenly incorporated. Oil and line a large baking tray (around 45 x 30 cm) with baking parchment then spoon in the cake mixture to a depth of around 2 cm. Bake for 20–25 minutes until firm. Remove from the oven and allow to cool, uncovered, overnight.

Passionfruit Curd
Place the passionfruit juice, cream, egg yolks and sugar in a large saucepan and stir until the sugar dissolves. Cook over a very gentle heat, stirring regularly, until the mixture thickens to coat the back of a spoon. This may take up to an hour, so be patient. Stir in the gelatine until completely dissolved, then strain the mixture through a fine sieve. Pour into a large shallow tray to a thickness of around 2 cm. Place in the refrigerator uncovered, and leave overnight until it sets firm.

Passionfruit Sauce
Place all the ingredients in a saucepan and bring to a gentle boil. Reduce the heat and simmer for around 45 minutes, or until the sauce is reduced by one-third. Strain the sauce and clean the passionfruit seeds under running water. Return them to the sauce and allow to cool.

To Serve
Preheat the grill to its highest temperature. Cut the dacquoise sponge into 6 x 10 cm squares. Cut the passionfruit curd into 6 x 10 cm squares. Arrange the sponge squares on a large baking tray and top each with a slice of curd. Sprinkle with the extra caster sugar and place under the grill until caramelised. Pour a generous amount of sauce onto each plate and carefully arrange the sponge squares on top. Serve straight away.

Serves 6

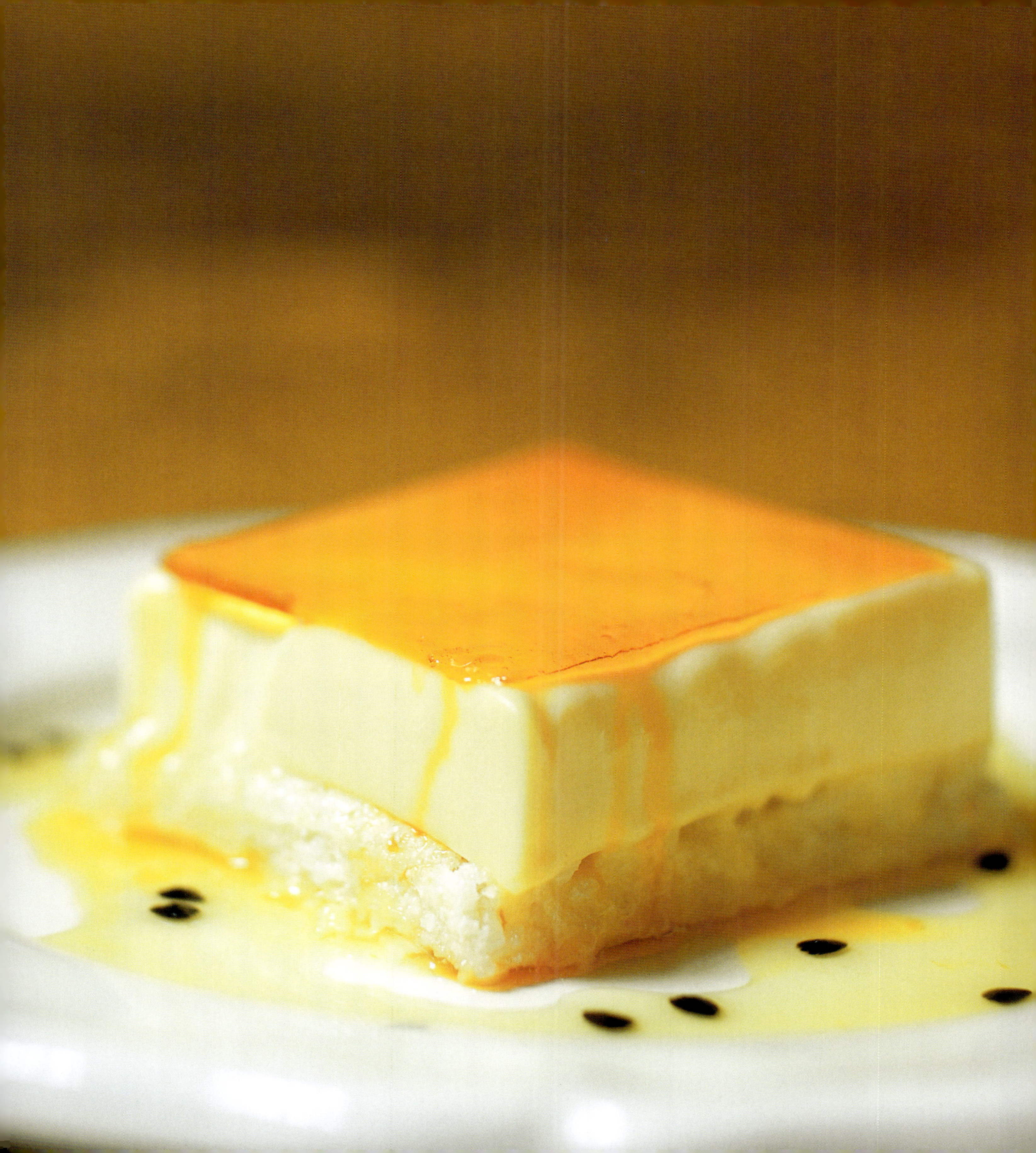

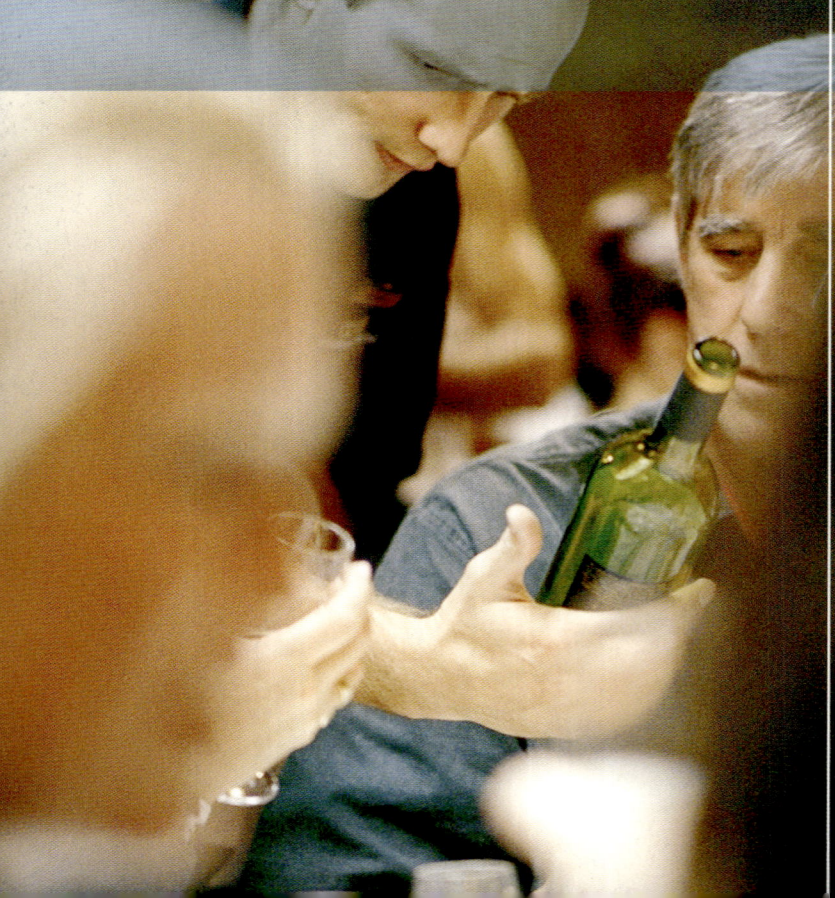

Winter in the Hunter Valley: the winds blow around the bare vines and the temperature plummets, but inside all is cosy and warm. It's a time for sitting by the fireside with a glass of red wine. It's a time for enjoying the fruits of the year and looking forward to the future.

winter

Beetroot Soup with Horseradish

Luke Mangan

2 medium–large beetroots
1 tablespoon butter
1 tablespoon extra-virgin olive oil
25 ml sherry vinegar
1 teaspoon horseradish relish,
  plus extra for serving
sea salt and freshly ground pepper

Peel the beetroot and slice into pieces about 5 mm wide. Heat the butter and extra-virgin olive oil in a heavy-based saucepan. Add the beetroot and toss to coat with the oil and butter. Cover the pan and cook on a very low heat for about an hour. Check at regular intervals to make sure the beetroot doesn't catch and burn.

Add the vinegar and simmer gently for a further 20 minutes. Remove from the heat and add 1 teaspoon of horseradish relish. Blend in a food processor until the soup is very smooth. It will be quite thick, and you may need to thin with 100 ml of water to achieve the desired consistency. Taste and adjust seasoning and refrigerate until ready to serve.

To Serve

Serve the soup, well-chilled, in shot glasses. Top with a tiny dollop of extra horseradish relish.

Serves 6

Offer a small glass of fino sherry to accompany these shot-glasses of chilled soup. It has the body and complex savoury flavours that will stand up to the strong earthiness of the beetroot flavours, and the sharpness of the horseradish.

Escalavida Terrine with Tapenade

Peter Doyle

Escalavida Terrine
6 eggplants, stalks removed and
  cut lengthwise into 1 cm slices
olive oil, for roasting
16 egg-shaped tomatoes,
  peeled, halved and seeded
3 sprigs thyme, steamed and chopped
salt and pepper
7 red capsicums, roasted and peeled

Garnish
4 tablespoons tapenade
4 tablespoons small black olives
2 tablespoons capers
extra-virgin olive oil
balsamic vinegar
sea salt and freshly ground black pepper

Escalavida Terrine
Preheat the oven to 175°C. Line a baking tray with baking parchment and brush with a little oil. Roast the eggplant for 12–15 minutes on each side. Remove from the oven and set aside to cool.

Lower the oven temperature to 125°C. Place a wire rack on a flat baking tray and arrange the tomato halves, cut side down, on the rack. Sprinkle with the thyme, salt and pepper and roast for 2 ½ hours, until the tomatoes have shrivelled and dried out. When the tomatoes are dry, remove from the oven and set aside to cool.

Line a small 30 cm terrine mould with cling film, allowing about 5 cm to hang over the sides. Cover the bottom of the mould with slices of eggplant, laid crosswise, letting them overlap slightly. Top with a layer of tomatoes and then another of eggplant. Cut the red capsicum to fit the mould and arrange a layer on top of the eggplant. Repeat the layering in this fashion to the top of the terrine mould, alternating eggplant between each layer of tomato and capsicum. Finish with a layer of red capsicums, then bring the cling film up over the top and seal. Weight the terrine down with a 2 kg weight (a small brick or a few tins or bottles will do quite well). Refrigerate overnight.

To Serve
Invert the terrine onto a cutting board and carefully lift off the mould and remove the cling film. Use a sharp knife to cut into slices 1–1.5 cm thick. Place a slice of terrine on each plate. Garnish each plate with a small spoonful of tapenade, some olives and capers. Drizzle a little olive oil and balsamic vinegar around the plate, sprinkle with sea salt and black pepper and serve with hot crusty bread.

Serves 6

Damien Pignolet

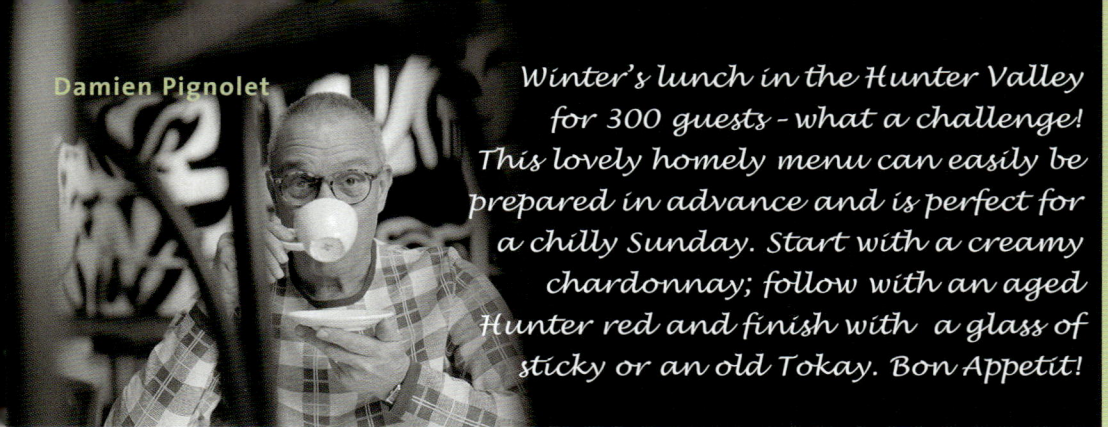

Winter's lunch in the Hunter Valley for 300 guests – what a challenge! This lovely homely menu can easily be prepared in advance and is perfect for a chilly Sunday. Start with a creamy chardonnay; follow with an aged Hunter red and finish with a glass of sticky or an old Tokay. Bon Appetit!

One of the legends of the Sydney food scene, Damien Pignolet has been a mentor to several generations of Australian chefs and he is highly regarded for his intelligent and precise approach to cooking. He first made his name at Claude's, a gastronomic jewel that epitomised classical French cuisine. Since 1993, Damien has been chef-owner of a second Sydney eating institution, Bistro Moncur. His menus feature all the favourite French bistro classics, albeit with the occasional modern Australian twist.

Celeriac Rémoulade with Fresh Crab and Rocket

1 bulb celeriac,
    (about 700–800 g) peeled
400 g fresh crab meat,
    large pieces broken up
120 g baby rocket leaves

Mayonnaise
1 small clove garlic, smashed
2 egg yolks
good pinch salt
freshly ground white pepper
1 heaped dessertspoon Dijon mustard
100 ml extra-virgin olive oil
120 ml olive or grapeseed oil
lemon juice to taste

Mayonnaise
Rub the inside of a small mixing bowl with the garlic and discard the pieces. Add the egg yolks, salt, pepper and mustard and whisk together until smooth. Add the oils a little at a time, whisking until the mixture emulsifies and thickens. Add lemon juice; taste and adjust seasonings.

Slice the celeriac very finely, using a mandolin (which is ideal) or a very sharp knife. Aim for slices about 5 mm thick. Cut the slices into even-sized julienne sticks and stir through enough mayonnaise to coat the celeriac without drowning it. Add the crab meat and mix together well.

To Serve
Use a pair of tongs to arrange high mounds of rémoulade on each plate and top with a small handful of rocket leaves.

Serves 6

Choose a creamy, full-bodied Chardonnay to soften the sharpness of the rocket and to enhance the nutty flavours of the celeriac and the sweetness of the crab.

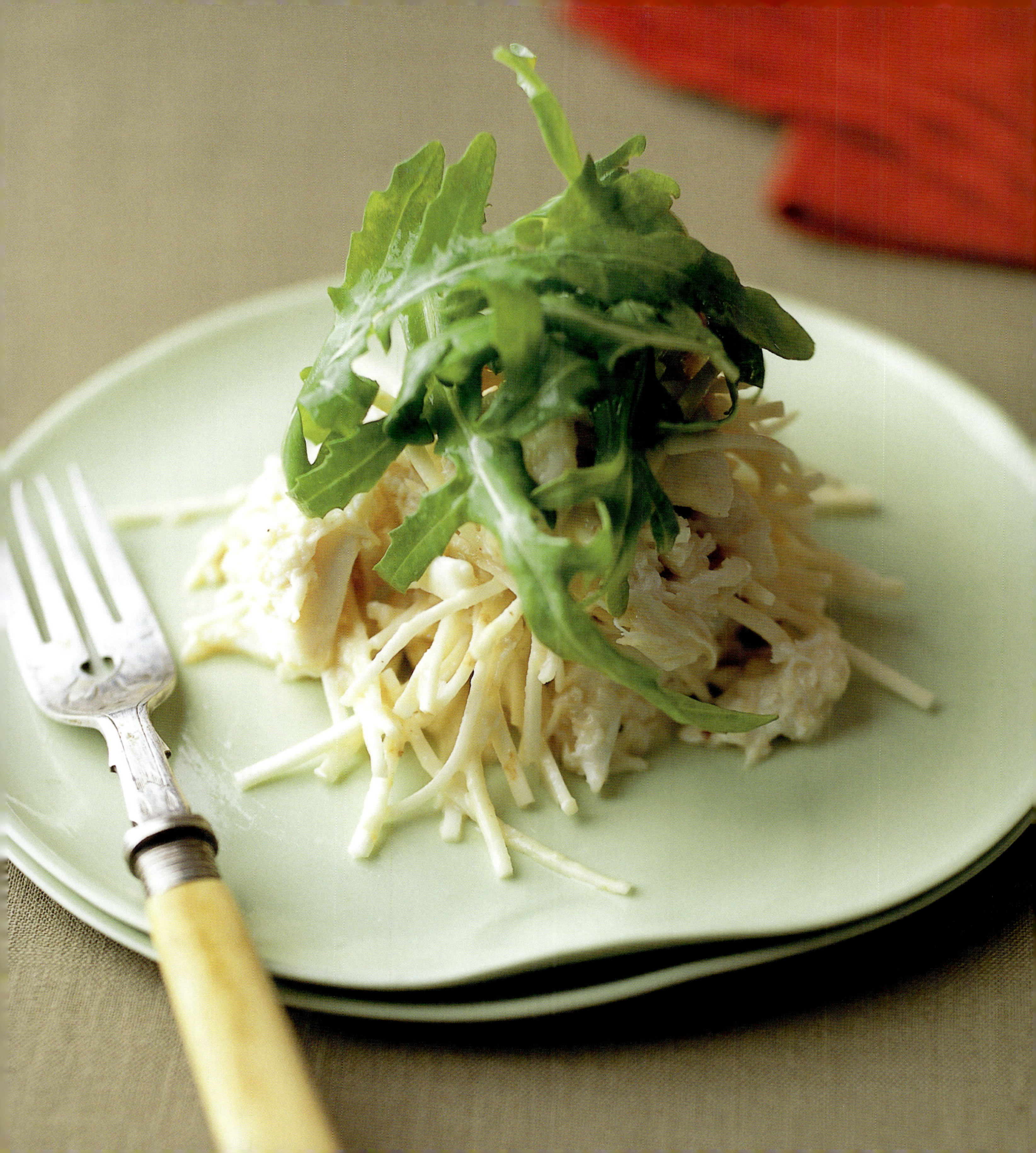

Grilled Tasmanian Half-Shell Scallops with Mediterranean Salsa

Gavin Cleary

24 Tasmanian half-shell scallops
80 ml olive oil
20 ml balsamic vinegar

Mediterranean Salsa
1 Spanish onion, chopped
1 red capsicum, chopped
1 continental cucumber, chopped
4 roma tomatoes, chopped
100 g kalamata olives,
    stoned and chopped

Salsa Dressing
1 tablespoon Dijon mustard
20 ml balsamic vinegar
100 ml olive oil

Salad Garnish
2 carrots
1 leek
100 g snowpea sprouts
1 bunch chives

Mediterranean Salsa
Place all the ingredients in a large mixing bowl and combine. Whisk together the dressing ingredients and stir into the salsa until nicely coated.

Salad Garnish
To make the salad garnish, use a sharp knife to shred the carrots and leeks into julienne strips (about 6 cm long). Cut the snowpea sprouts and chives into 6 cm lengths. Mix together well.

To Serve
Preheat the grill to its highest temperature. Place the scallops on a baking tray. Whisk together the olive oil and vinegar and drizzle over the scallops. Place under the grill for 3 minutes then top with a teaspoon of the salsa and return to the grill for another 2 minutes.

Place a small mound of salad garnish in the centre of each plate. Arrange the scallop shells around the sides, allowing 4 per person.

Serves 6

A Riesling, with subtle, fresh fruit flavours and cleansing acidity will complement the rich sweetness of the scallops and stand up to the sharpness of the salsa dressing.

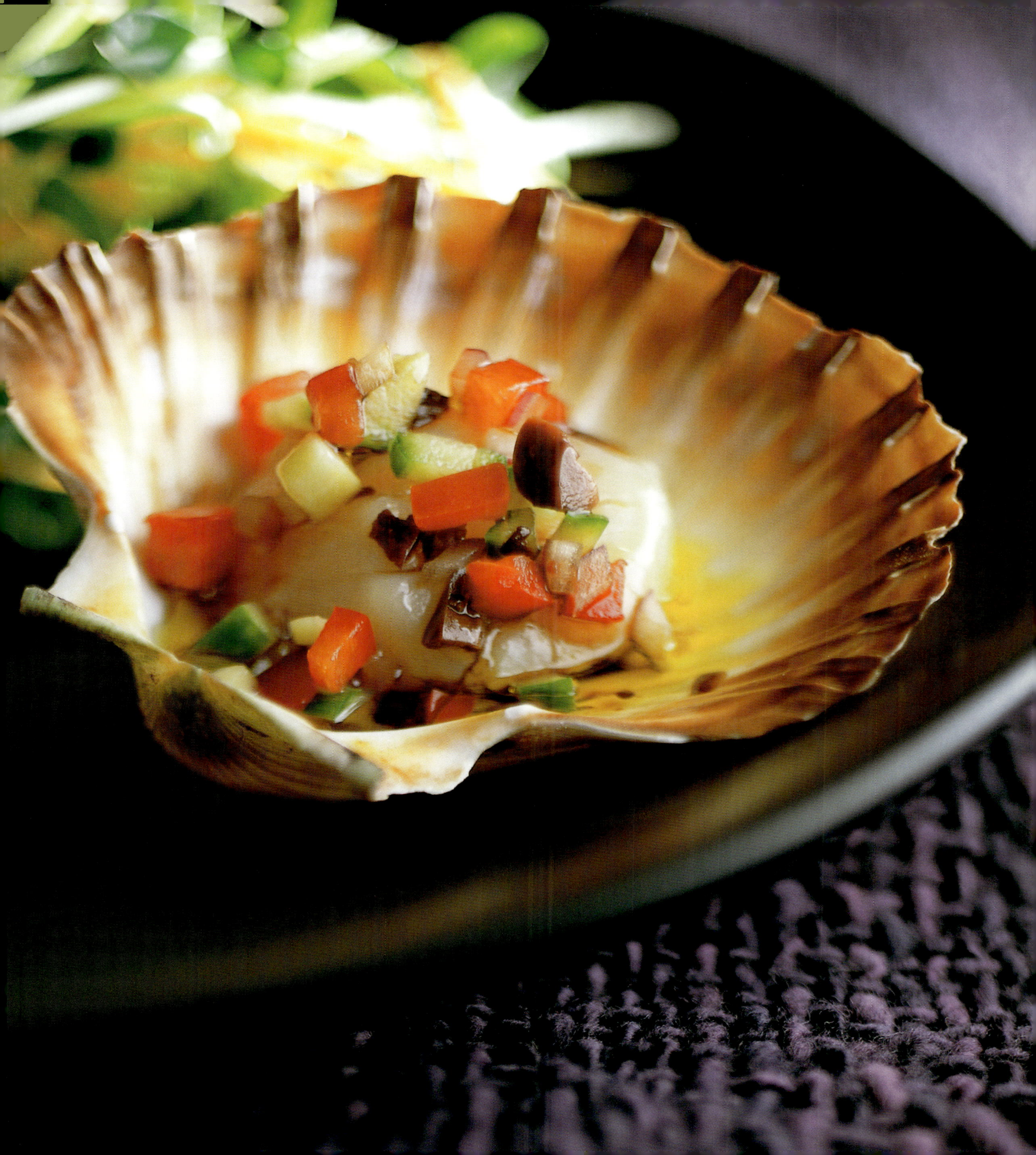

Raw Salmon with Soy, Ginger and Shallot Dressing

Luke Mangan

The pickled ginger requires a minimum of 2 days to 'pickle', and can happily be stored in the fridge for up to 3 months.

300 g salmon, thinly sliced
120 g goat's cheese, crumbled
3 big handfuls of rocket
sea salt and freshly ground pepper

Pickled Ginger
300 g fresh ginger, peeled and finely sliced
750 ml water
250 g caster sugar
150 ml white wine vinegar (or more, to taste)

Ginger and Shallot Dressing
6 shallots, peeled and finely chopped
300 g pickled ginger, finely chopped
20 ml olive oil
1 tablespoon soy sauce

Pickled Ginger
To pickle the ginger, bring a saucepan of cold water to the boil and blanch the ginger for 20 seconds, then refresh in cold water. Repeat 3 times to extract any bitterness from the ginger.

In another small non-reactive saucepan mix together the water, sugar and vinegar. Bring to the boil, making sure the sugar dissolves completely. Pour the boiling liquid onto the ginger and allow to cool. Transfer to an airtight jar and store in the fridge.

Ginger and Shallot Dressing
Mix all the ingredients together and leave for an hour for the flavours to infuse.

To Serve
Arrange the thinly sliced salmon on each plate and top with a small mound of rocket and some crumbled goat's cheese. Season with salt and pepper and drizzle over a little dressing just before serving.

Serves 6

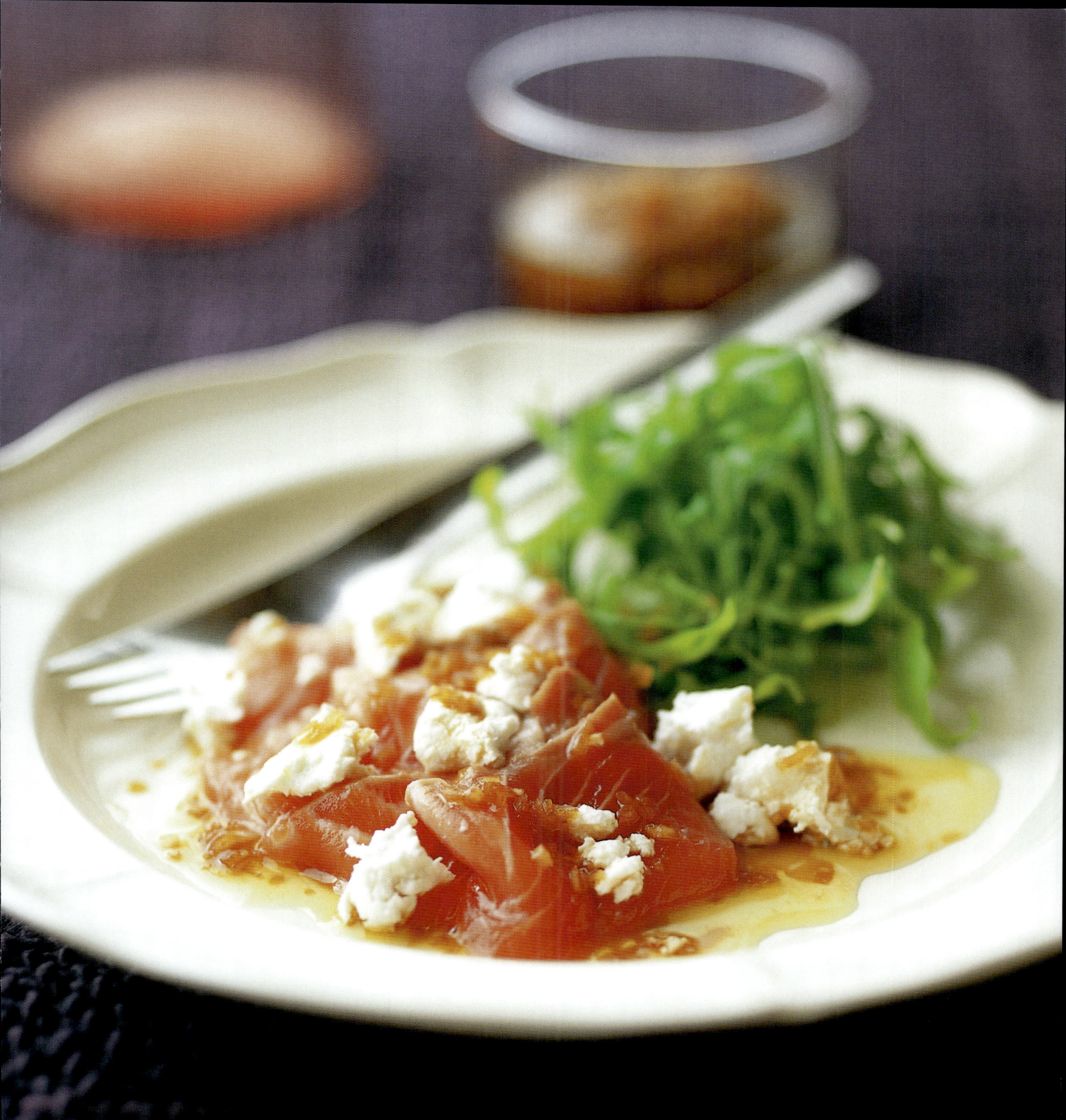

Confit of Ocean Trout with Baba Ghanoush and Preserved Lemon Oil

Matthew Moran

6 x 80 g ocean trout fillets,
    skin and bones removed
2 litres olive oil

Baba Ghanoush
2 large eggplants (about 500 g each)
1 clove garlic, finely chopped
2 teaspoons lemon juice
1 tablespoon tahini
2 teaspoons olive oil
salt and pepper

Preserved Lemon Oil
10 g preserved lemon,
    rind only, white pith removed
90 ml extra-virgin olive oil
40 ml lemon juice

Garnish
sea salt
30 g ocean trout roe
18 leaves baby basil, to garnish

Confit of Ocean Trout
Preheat the oven to 50°C. Fit a wire rack into the bottom of a large deep baking tray. Arrange the ocean trout fillets on the rack and pour in the olive oil (the fish should be compeletely immersed in the oil). Place in the oven and cook for 20–25 minutes, or until the fish is just starting to turn opaque; be careful not to overcook it. Remove the fish from the oil, drain well and keep at room temperature until ready to serve.

Baba Ghanoush
To make the baba ghanoush, preheat the oven to 180°C. Roast the eggplants for about an hour, or until completely soft. When they are soft, chargrill them briefly to give a smoky flavour (this can be done directly on the naked flame of your stove burners). When cool enough to handle, peel away and discard the skin. Place the pulp in a food processor with the remaining ingredients and process until smooth. Taste and adjust seasonings if desired.

Preserved Lemon Oil
To make the preserved lemon oil, slice the preserved lemon finely and mix with the extra-virgin olive oil and lemon juice.

To Serve
Place a neat spoonful of baba ghanoush in the centre of each plate and arrange a piece of confit trout on top. Drizzle the preserved lemon oil over the fish and around the plate. Season lightly with salt and garnish with ocean trout roe and basil leaves.

Serves 6

Crepinette of Duck and Confit Duck with Flageolet Beans and Truffle Oil and Beetroot Purée

Damien Pignolet

Caul fat is a fatty pork membrane used to encase the duck rissoles. It dissolves during cooking, but holds the filling together. It is available from most butchers. Confit (preserved duck) and truffle oil are both available from good delicatessens.

Duck Crepinettes
400 g skinless boned duck breasts
300 g lean pork, shoulder or neck
200 g pork back fat (from the loin)
300 g boneless confit duck
   (about 450 g bone in)
3 teaspoons salt
1/4 teaspoon freshly ground black pepper
1/4 teaspoon ground nutmeg
1/2 teaspoon ground allspice
pinch of ground ginger
1 small clove garlic, crushed
1 tablespoon brandy
250 g caul fat, soaked in
   cold salted water for 1 hour
olive oil for frying

Beetroot Purée
5 medium beetroots
3 roma tomatoes
splash of olive oil
salt and pepper

Flageolet Beans with Truffle Oil
600–700 g canned flageolet
   or cannellini beans
1/2 teaspoon truffle oil, or more to taste
1 dessertspoon extra-virgin olive oil
salt and pepper to taste

Garnish
1 cup small sage leaves
olive oil for frying

Duck Crepinettes
Dice the duck breasts, pork and pork fat into small pieces then mince coarsely. Mince a third of this again. Roughly dice the confit duck into even pieces. Mix all the meat and fat together with the salt, spices, garlic and brandy. Use your hand to work the mixture until it feels greasy and forms threads between the fingers.

Drain the caul and rinse under cold running water. Squeeze gently and lay on a work surface. Use a sharp knife to cut into 6 pieces. Divide the meat into 6 rissoles, about 3 cm thick. Lay each on a piece of caul fat and trim to allow just enough caul to wrap them. Transfer onto an oiled rack and refrigerate for several hours before cooking.

Preheat the oven to 160°C. Heat the olive oil in a heavy-based ovenproof pan. Fry the crepinettes on a gentle heat, turning so they colour evenly all over. Transfer to the oven and cook for 15 minutes, or until the juices run clear when pierced with a skewer.

Beetroot Purée
Preheat the oven to 160°C. Wash beetroots and trim all but 2 cm of stalk. Wrap each beetroot in foil and bake for 40–60 minutes until tender. Remove from the oven, peel and allow to cool. When cool, dice them evenly. Place the tomatoes on a baking tray, drizzle with oil and roast until they start to brown and collapse. Pass them through a fine sieve. Process the beetroot with enough tomato to make a smooth purée that holds its shape. Season to taste.

When ready to serve, heat a cast-iron griddle pan or heavy-based frying pan and gently reheat the crepinettes. Warm the beans and add the oils and seasonings. Reheat the beetroot purée (Easily done in a microwave oven). Heat the olive oil in a small frying pan and fry the sage leaves until crisp. Drain on absorbent paper.

To Serve
Divide the beans between 6 plates, making a small well in the middle. Fill with a spoonful of beetroot purée, lay a crepinette on top and scatter with sage leaves.

Serves 6

Pan-Fried Barramundi with Globe Artichoke, Asparagus and Spinach and Rich Shiraz Jus

Gavin Cleary

200 g globe artichokes,
    preserved in oil
    (stems attached if possible)
12 asparagus spears
400 g spinach, well washed
100 ml olive oil
6 x 220 g barramundi fillets
salt and freshly ground white pepper

Shiraz Jus
1 tablespoon butter
50 ml olive oil
1 white onion, diced small
5 cloves garlic, crushed
300 ml shiraz
800 ml good quality beef stock
salt and pepper

Shiraz Jus
Heat the butter and olive oil in a heavy-based frying pan. Add the onion and garlic and sauté over a low heat until soft and translucent. Be careful not to burn the garlic as it will turn bitter. Add the red wine, turn up the heat and cook until reduced by a quarter. Add the beef stock and return to the boil. Lower the heat and simmer until reduced by half. Season to taste then pass through a fine sieve.

Prepare the vegetables. Cut the artichokes into quarters lengthwise. Snap the woody ends off the asparagus and blanch them in boiling water for 45 seconds. Refresh in iced water.

Heat half the olive oil and sauté the artichoke and asparagus for 2–3 minutes, or until tender. Towards the end of the cooking time, add the spinach and turn it in the pan until it wilts and softens.

Meanwhile, season the barramundi fillets. Heat the remaining olive oil in a large heavy-based frying pan. Fry the barramundi for about 4 minutes, until a nice golden colour. Turn carefully and fry on the other side for a further 4 minutes, or until cooked through.

To Serve
Gently warm through the shiraz jus. Place a spoonful of sautéed vegetables in the centre of each plate. Top with a barramundi fillet. Drizzle the shiraz jus around the edge of the plate and serve straight away.

Serves 6

Shiraz would be an interesting, if unconventional match to this white fish dish. Barramundi is a robust flavoured fish and here it is teamed with strongly flavoured vegetables – it will stand up well to a full-bodied wine such as Shiraz.

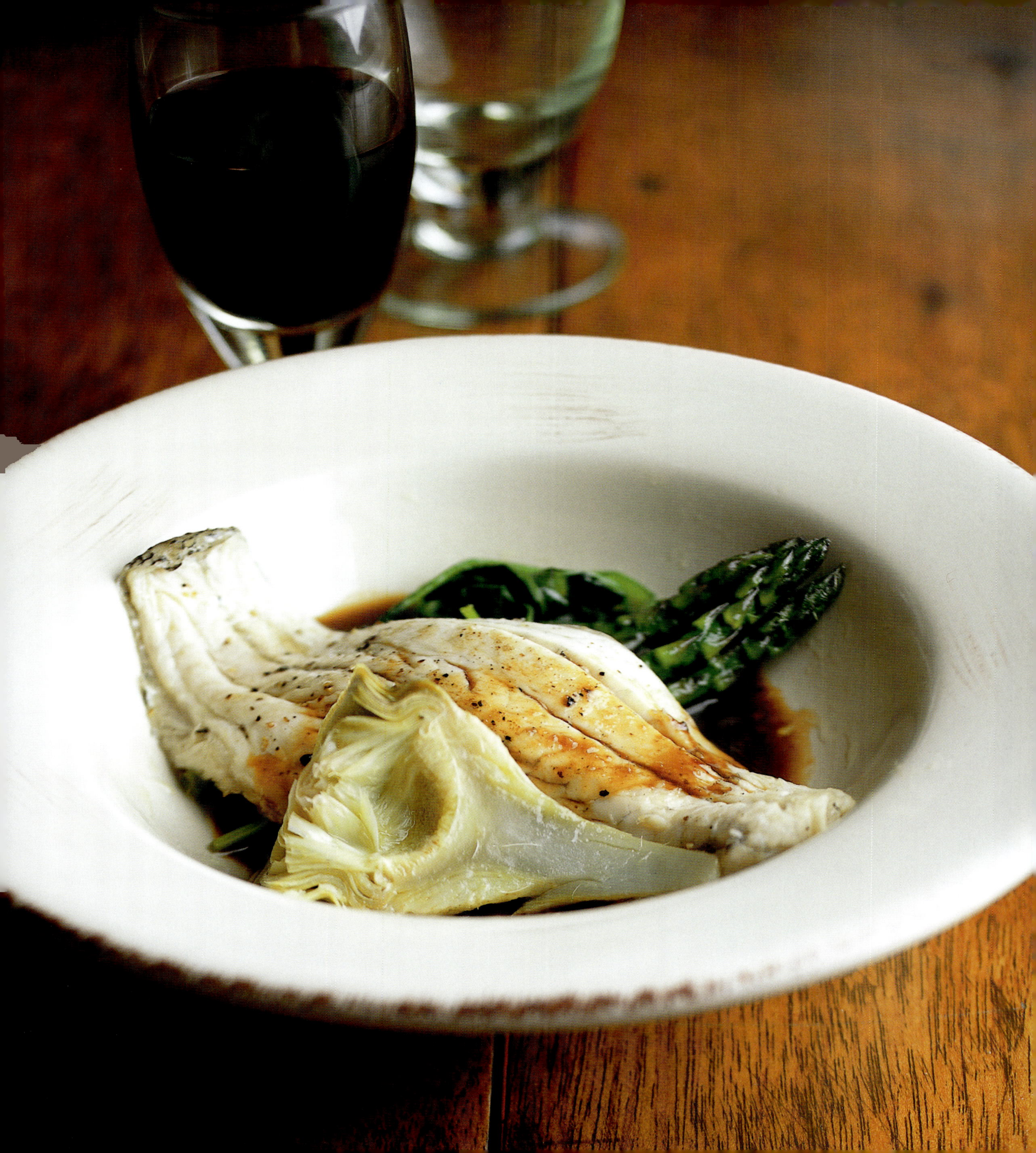

Chicken Riviera with Nicoise Potatoes and Fennel Sauce

Mark Best

The potatoes in this dish are cooked with Nicoise and Riviera olives. These are small, dark brown olives originally from the French and Italian Riviera.

2 x 1.5 kg chickens
salt and pepper
extra-virgin olive oil

Fennel Sauce
1 large head of fennel
50 ml extra-virgin olive oil
150 ml white wine
salt and freshly
　ground white pepper
200 ml chicken stock
40 g butter
juice of ½ a lemon

Nicoise Potatoes
600 g nicola potatoes, peeled
a few sprigs rosemary,
　roughly chopped
a handful of sage leaves,
　roughly chopped
250 g Nicoise and Riviera olives,
　stoned
salt and freshly ground
　white pepper

Fennel Sauce
Preheat the oven to 180°C. Trim the fennel and slice thinly. Arrange the sliced fennel in a deep baking tray. Pour on the oil and white wine and season with salt and pepper. Bake for about 40 minutes, until the fennel is soft and translucent. Remove from the oven and tip into a blender. Blend to a smooth purée then taste and adjust seasonings if necessary. Push the purée through a fine sieve and reserve until you are ready to serve.

When you are ready to serve, bring the chicken stock to the boil, whisk in the butter and lemon juice then add the fennel purée and mix together. Adjust seasonings and keep warm.

Roast Chickens
Turn up the oven temperature to 220°C. Season the chickens and rub with extra-virgin olive oil. Roast for an hour, or until the juices run clear when the thick part of the leg is pierced with a skewer.

Nicoise Potatoes
Cut the potatoes into neat 2 cm dice. Blanch them quickly in boiling salted water then drain and leave for a few minutes to steam dry. Add the herbs and olives and season with salt and pepper. Pour on the olive oil and toss well so that the potatoes are nicely coated in oil. Tip into a baking tray and roast in the oven with the chickens for 15–20 minutes, or until the potatoes are a lovely golden brown.

To Serve
Carve the chicken and divide the meat between 6 plates. Serve with a generous mound of potatoes. Pour the fennel sauce around the chicken. Drizzle over a little extra-virgin olive oil and serve straight away.

Serves 6

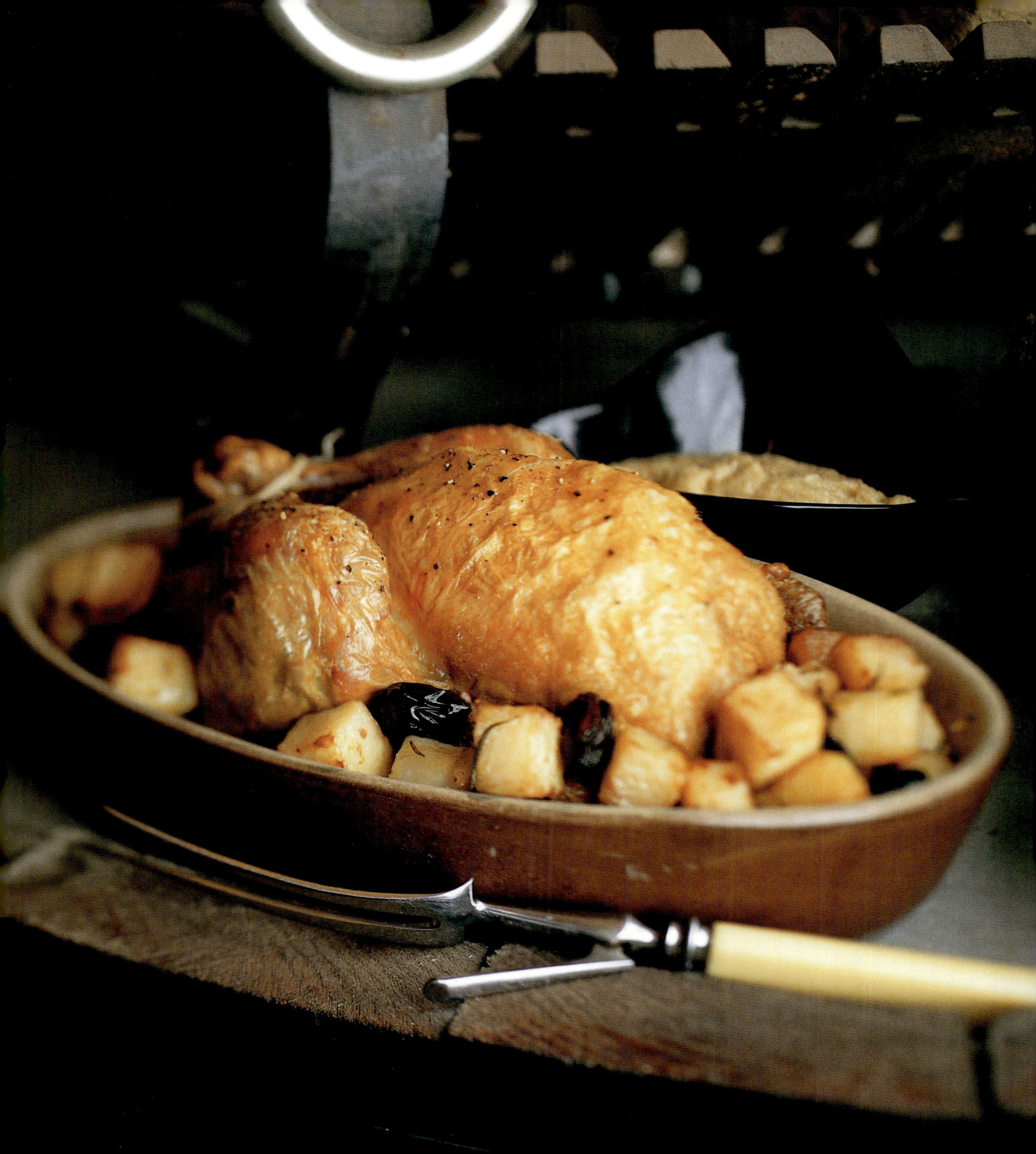

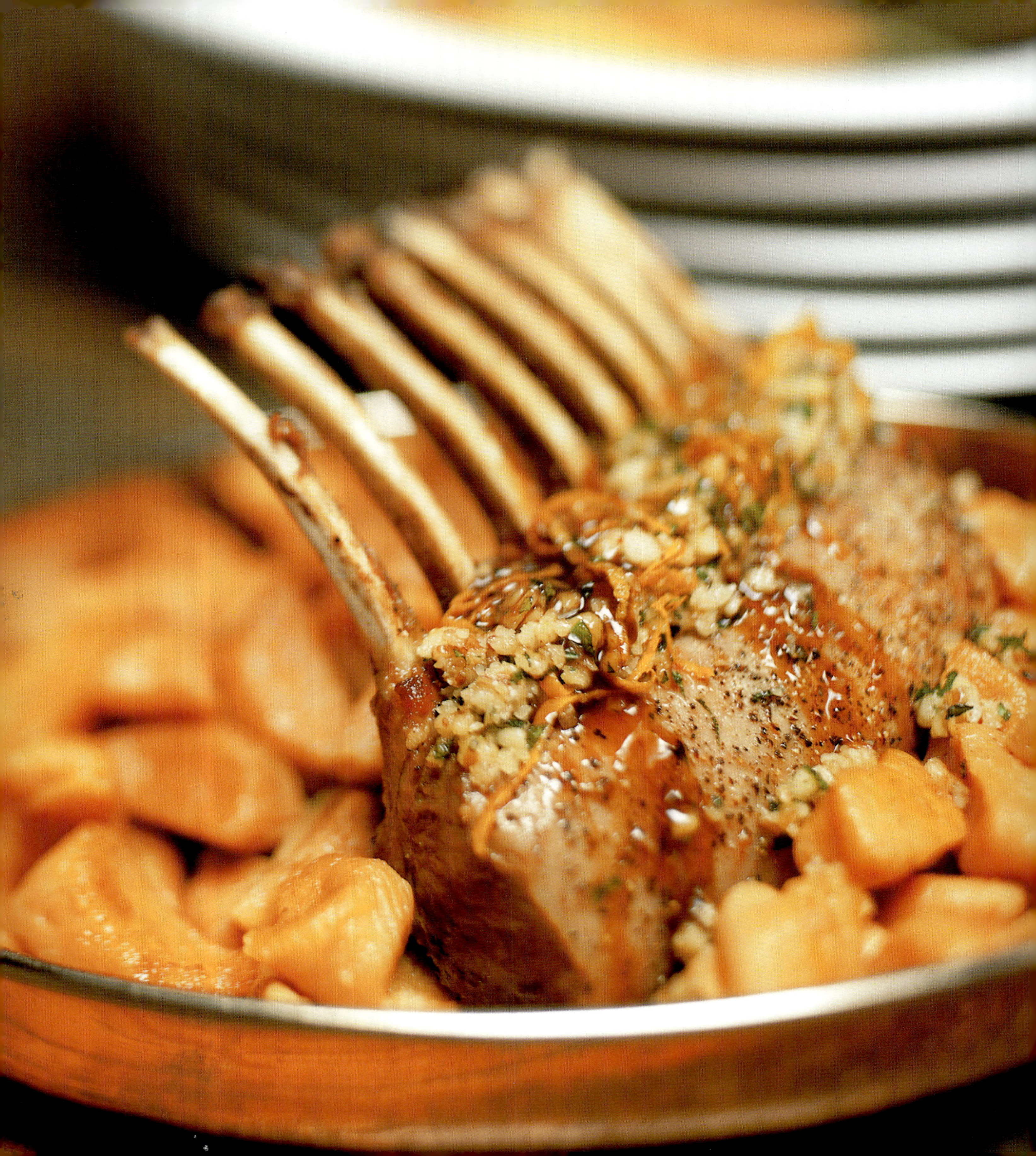

Wild Pepper-Crusted Lamb with Pacific Gnocchi and Mint Gremolata

Michael James

This dish uses horopito, a native New Zealand pepper that adds a lovely zestiness to the lamb. Lemon myrtle makes a good alternative. Kumara and taro are both starchy tubers (a little like yams) found in the South Pacific.

3 x 8 point lamb racks
1 teaspoon horopito
salt
2 tablespoons olive oil
200 ml lamb jus

Pacific Gnocchi
500 g golden kumara, steamed until tender and peeled
500 g taro, steamed until tender and peeled
100 g plain flour
2 egg yolks
salt and pepper
1 tablespoon butter
1 tablespoon olive oil

Mint Gremolata
50 g macadamia nuts
50 g pecan nuts
½ cup mint leaves, finely chopped
grated zest of 1 orange
salt and pepper
100 ml olive oil

Pacific Gnocchi
Push the warm kumara and taro through a potato ricer or food mill directly onto a clean work surface. Add the flour and egg yolks and knead quickly to a smooth dough, making sure the flour and eggs are thoroughly incorporated. You may need to add extra flour if the kumara has absorbed too much liquid during the steaming. Roll the dough tightly in baking paper to form a tube approx 3 cm in diameter. Cut the dough into equal-sized pieces. Use the tines of a fork dipped in flour to mark each gnocchi.

Bring a pot of water to a rolling boil and add the gnocchi. As they rise to the surface remove from the water and refresh in iced water. Melt the butter and olive oil in a large frying pan. Fry the gnocchi on both sides until golden brown. Drain on absorbent paper and keep warm until ready to serve.

Mint Gremolata
Put the nuts into a food processor and chop finely. Remove from the blender and add the finely chopped mint leaves and orange zest. Season with salt and pepper and mix in the oil.

Wild Pepper-Crusted Lamb
Preheat the oven to 200°C. Season the lamb racks with the horopito and salt. Drizzle the olive oil in a baking tray, add the lamb racks and roast for 8 minutes for medium-rare. Remove from the oven and leave to rest in a warm place for a further 10 minutes.

To Serve
Gently heat the lamb jus to make a sauce. Arrange some gnocchi in the centre of each plate. Slice each lamb rack into quarters and stack two on top of each serve of gnocchi with a dollop of gremolata. Drizzle the plate with some sauce and serve straight away. This dish is good served with wood-roasted carrots or crisp green beans.

Serves 6

A Merlot, with soft approachable fruit characters, will complement the sweet-starchiness of the gnocchi and the lamb and not detract from the minty citrus flavours of the gremolata.

Luke Mangan

My food philosophy is ultimate simplicity! We have an amazing wealth of produce available in Australia; let the ingredients speak for themselves.

Luke Mangan is one of Australia's best known chefs and food entrepreneurs, with four Sydney restaurants and bars to his name. His award-winning food is contemporary and stylish – his flagship restaurant Salt was voted Best Restaurant in 2000 and has two Chef's Hats. Luke is the author of two cookbooks, *BLD* and *Luke Mangan Food*, and he is the food editor for the *Sydney Morning Herald* and *Melbourne Age* newspapers. He appears regularly on Australian television and in 2003 he won the Chef's category in the *GQ* magazine Men of the Year Awards.

Poached Fillet of Beef with Mushroom Custard and Caramelised Witlof

1.3 kg fillet of beef
sea salt
3 litres beef stock
handful of shiitake
　mushrooms, diced

Mushroom Custard
500 g button mushrooms
100 g shiitake mushrooms
1 tablespoon butter
500 ml pouring cream
pinch salt
3 eggs
2 egg yolks

Caramelised Witlof
75 g butter
100 g sugar
4 heads witlof,
　cut in half lengthwise
100 ml beef stock

Trim off any excess fat and white sinew strips from the beef. Sprinkle with salt and seal in a hot pan until it is evenly coloured all over. Take out of the pan and rest until cool. When cool wrap in plastic film to create a tight cylinder and tie the ends. Rest in the fridge for 4 hours.

When nearly ready to serve, place the beef stock in a large saucepan and bring to a rolling boil. Unwrap the beef, place it in the stock and cook for 15 minutes, making sure the stock boils continuously. Remove the beef and keep warm until ready to serve. Continue to boil the stock until it has reduced by one-third.

Mushroom Custard
Cut the mushrooms into quarters, wash well and drain. Melt the butter in a pan and slowly cook the mushrooms until the liquid has evaporated. Add the cream and simmer until reduced by one-third. Season with salt. Blend to a smooth purée, then strain the mix through a sieve. Put in the fridge to chill. Mix the eggs and egg yolks together and stir into the cold mushroom mix. Taste and adjust seasoning if necessary.

Meanwhile, lightly oil 6 dariole moulds, and pour in enough custard to half-fill them. Place the moulds in a steamer and steam for 10 minutes. Remove from the heat and allow to rest.

Caramelised Witlof
Melt the butter and sugar in a saucepan over low heat, stirring continuously until sugar has dissolved and a light caramel has formed. Add the witlof and stock and cook until the witlof has softened.

To Serve
Blanch the diced shiitake mushrooms in a little boiling stock. Carefully unmould each custard and place on each plate at 12 o'clock. Arrange a small amount of witlof to the right-hand side of the plate and some slices of beef on the left. Scatter the plate with a few mushrooms and drizzle the mushroom sauce around the outside.

Serves 6

Try an aged Cabernet Sauvignon with this beef. Its smooth rich fruit characters will go perfectly with the creamy mushroom custard and will soften the underlying bitterness of the witlof.

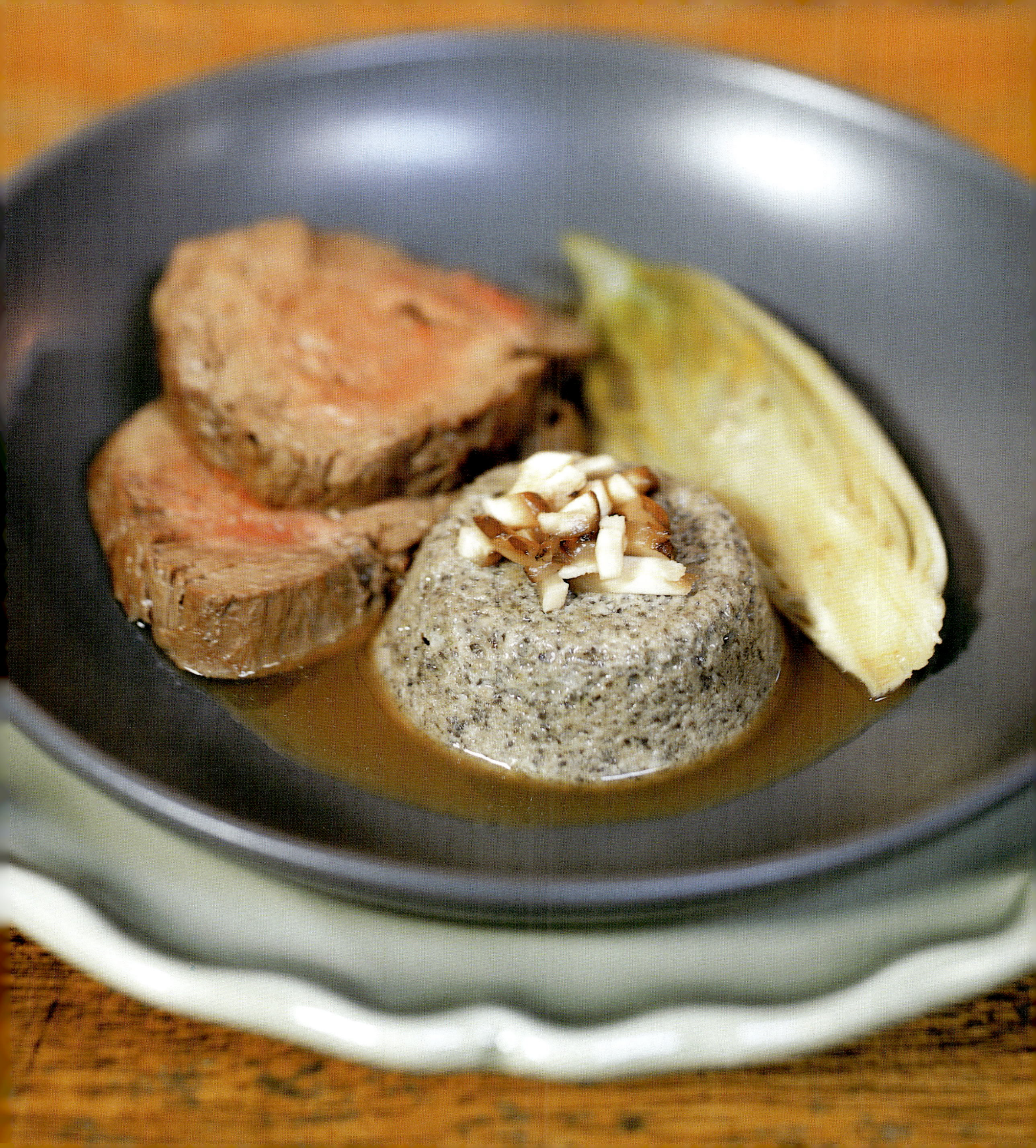

Prime Beef Tenderloin on Spinach with Vintner's Butter

Peter Doyle

6 x 200 g pieces beef fillet
100 ml olive oil
salt and pepper to season
100 g butter
300 g spinach, well washed, stems removed
150 ml reduced veal stock

Vintner's Butter
60 g golden shallots, chopped
250 ml white wine
2 tablespoons tarragon, chopped
12 anchovy fillets
1 teaspoon crushed garlic
2 tablespoons Dijon mustard
40 ml lemon juice
40 ml brandy
40 ml Worcestershire sauce
600 g softened butter
salt and pepper

Vintner's Butter
Place the chopped shallots in a heavy-based frying pan with the white wine and tarragon. Simmer until the liquid has reduced to about 50 ml. Place the shallot mixture into a food processor with the anchovies, garlic and mustard. Blend well, then add the lemon juice, brandy and Worcestershire sauce and blend again. Add the butter, salt and pepper and process again until well blended. Scrape the butter out onto a sheet of cling film and roll into a log. Refrigerate or freeze until required, but serve at room temperature.

Beef Tenderloin
Preheat your grill, griddle or barbecue to its highest temperature. Brush each piece of beef fillet with a little olive oil and season with salt and pepper. For medium–rare, sear the beef for about 2–3 minutes on each side, not forgetting the sides (i.e. a total of 8–12 minutes). Remove from the heat and allow to rest in a warm place for about 5 minutes.

Spinach
Melt the butter in a large heavy-based frying pan. Add the spinach and toss over the heat until it wilts and softens. Season and keep warm until ready to serve.

To Serve
Warm the veal stock to serve as a sauce. Divide the spinach evenly between each plate. Place the rested steak next to the spinach and top with a slice of vintner's butter. Drizzle a little sauce around the plate and serve straight away.

Serves 6

Choose a full-bodied Cabernet Sauvignon or Shiraz to match the salty-sharp flavours of the vintner's butter and the strong iron flavours of the beef and spinach.

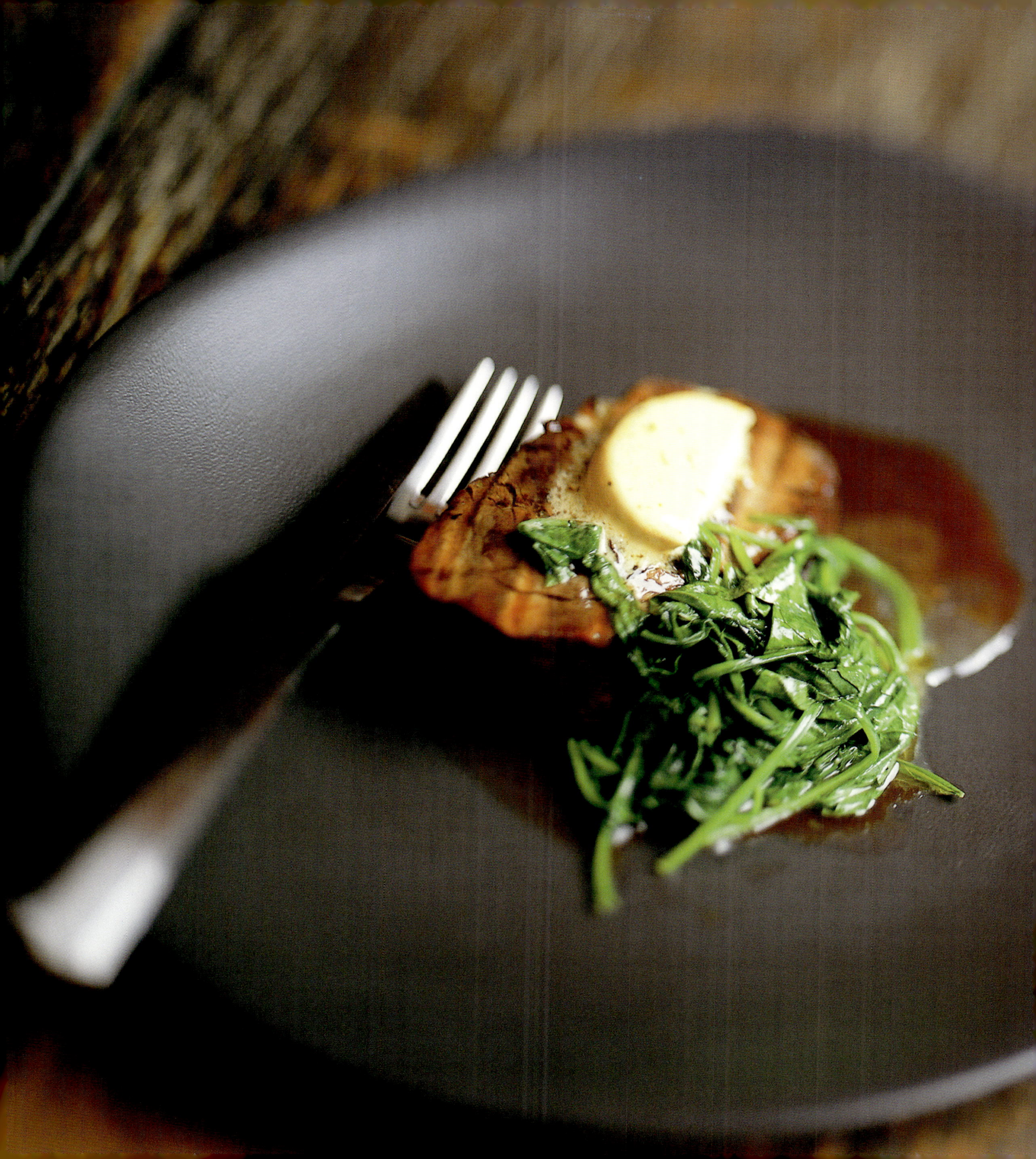

Candied Orange Rice with Buttered Almonds and Baked Rhubarb Sauce

Damien Pignolet

This is a variation on a wonderful Danish Christmas dessert that came to me via my former business partner, Mogens Bay Esbensen, when we operated Pavilion On The Park. Serve in individual dishes or in a big glass bowl and let the guests help themselves!

Candied Orange Rice
700 ml milk
a good pinch salt
75 g sugar
½ vanilla bean,
　split lengthwise and seeds scraped
120 g short-grain rice
350 ml thickened cream
80 g candied oranges, finely diced
80 g unsalted butter
120 g flaked almonds

Baked Rhubarb Sauce
1 bunch rhubarb,
　trimmed and washed
75 g sugar
2 tablespoons water
icing sugar
zest and juice of 1 lemon or lime

Candied Orange Rice
Combine the milk, salt, sugar, vanilla bean and seeds in a medium-sized saucepan and heat gently. Stir to dissolve the sugar then bring to the boil. Lower the heat, stir in the rice and cover the surface with a circle of baking parchment. Cook slowly for 20 minutes, or until the rice is tender.

Tip the rice into a wide bowl and leave until it has cooled to room temperature, stirring from time to time. When the rice is cool, cover the surface with a fresh piece of baking parchment and chill in the refrigerator for 30 minutes (don't allow it to set firm).

Whip the cream to firm peaks and fold into the rice with the diced orange pieces. Transfer to a glass serving bowl, cover and chill.

Baked Rhubarb Sauce
Preheat the oven to 160°C. Cut the rhubarb into even pieces. Toss with the sugar and tip into a medium-sized, ovenproof dish. Sprinkle with the water and bake in the oven until tender, about 30 minutes.

Purée until smooth and adjust sweetness to taste with icing sugar. Stir in a little lemon zest and juice, again, to taste.

To Serve
Melt the butter in a medium-sized, heavy-based frying pan. Add the flaked almonds and cook over a medium flame, turning constantly so they don't burn. Tip into a sieve and drain well, then transfer them to a clean tea towel to dry. Scatter the almonds over the candied orange rice and serve accompanied by the rhubarb sauce.

Serves 6

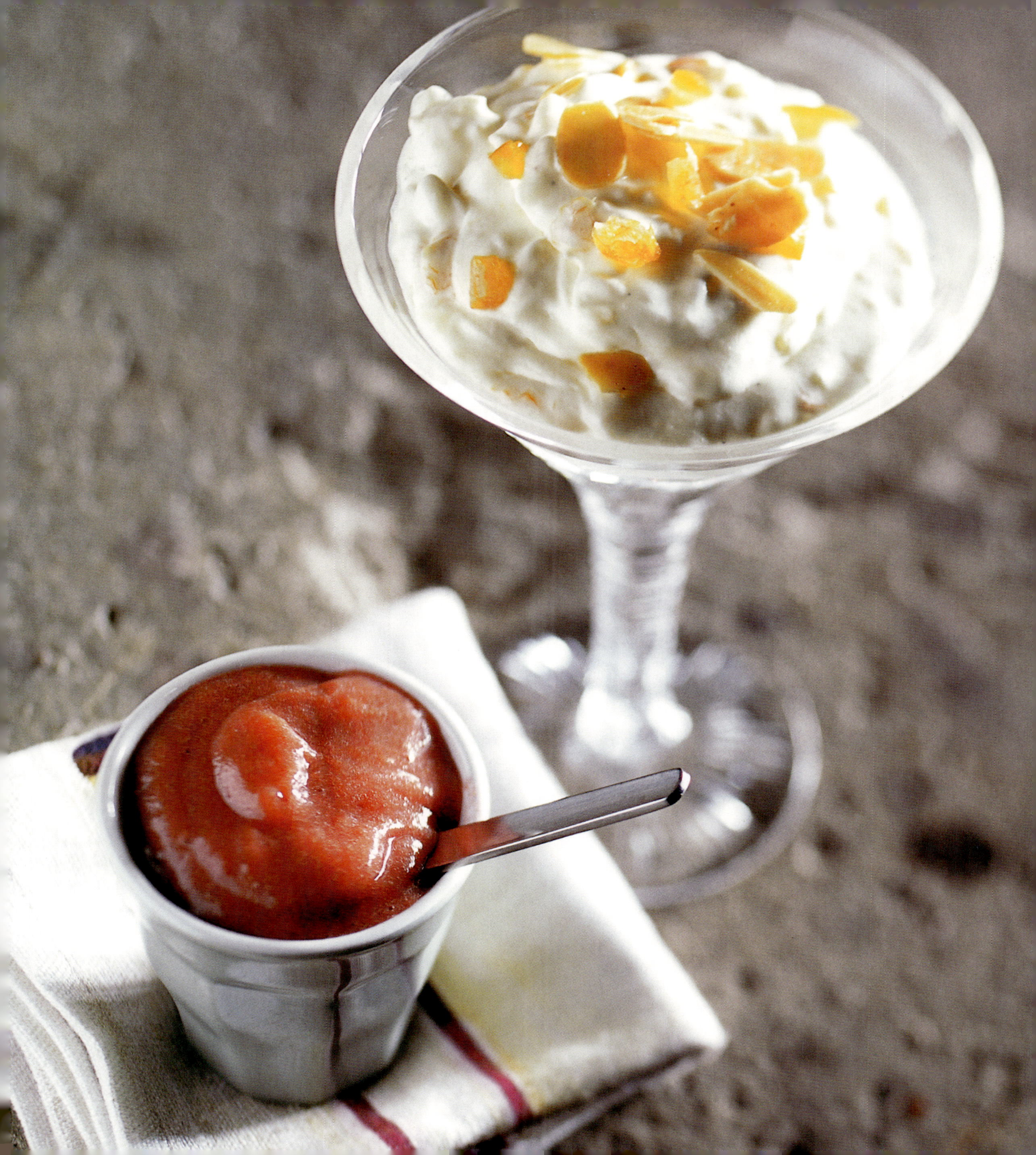

Apple Galette with Muscatel Compote and Crème Anglaise

Mark Best

The shortbread pastry tart-bases may be made up to 2 days before you want to serve them.

3 golden delicious apples, peeled and cored
icing sugar to dust

Shortbread Pastry
250 g plain flour
50 g cornflour
100 g caster sugar
1 vanilla bean, split and scraped
200 g chilled unsalted butter, roughly diced

Crème Anglaise
500 ml milk
500 ml thickened cream
130 g caster sugar
1 vanilla bean, split and scraped
12 egg yolks

Muscatel Compote
500 g dried muscatel grapes
250 g caster sugar
250 ml water
100 ml calvados or apple brandy
zest of ½ lemon

Shortbread Pastry
Put the dry ingredients into a food processor and blend briefly. Add the seeds from the vanilla pod and the chilled butter. Blend until the pastry just starts to come together. Tip out onto a sheet of cling film, wrap and refrigerate for 30 minutes. Dust the work surface with icing sugar and roll the pastry out to a 5 mm thickness. Cut into 6 circles 8 cm in diameter. Re-roll any offcuts, chill and use them as well. Refrigerate the pastry discs for a minimum of 1 hour.

Preheat the oven to 170°C. Transfer the pastry discs to non-stick baking sheets and bake for 8–10 minutes, or until golden brown. Store in an airtight container until ready to serve.

Crème Anglaise
Put milk, cream, sugar and vanilla bean into a heavy-based saucepan and heat gently until the sugar dissolves. Whisk the yolks until they are pale and creamy. Pour on the hot cream, whisking continuously. Return the custard to a clean pan and heat very gently until it thickens. Do not allow to boil.

Muscatel Compote
Remove stalks from muscatels; rinse fruit well. Put the sugar, water and calvados in a heavy-based saucepan and heat gently until the sugar dissolves. Add zest and boil for 1 minute. Add the muscatels, lower the heat and simmer for 10 minutes. Remove from heat and leave to cool.

When Ready To Serve
Preheat the oven to 200°C. Cut the apples into fine (1 mm) slices and fan them out to form 10 cm circles on a non-stick baking sheet. Bake for about 10 minutes, or until the apples start to colour and soften. Remove from the oven and set aside (they may be prepared to this stage up to 3 hours ahead of time). An hour before you are ready to serve, dust the apple circles heavily with icing sugar and caramelise with a blow torch or under a very hot grill.

Arrange a shortbread base in the centre of each dessert plate. Use a wide spatula to lift the caramelised apple circles onto the shortbread and spoon over the muscatel compote. Pour some crème anglaise around the tart and serve straight away.

Serves 6

This is a rich and complex dessert. The intense raisin flavours of a Liqueur Tokay will enhance the sweet caramelised apple and the fruitiness of the muscatel compote.

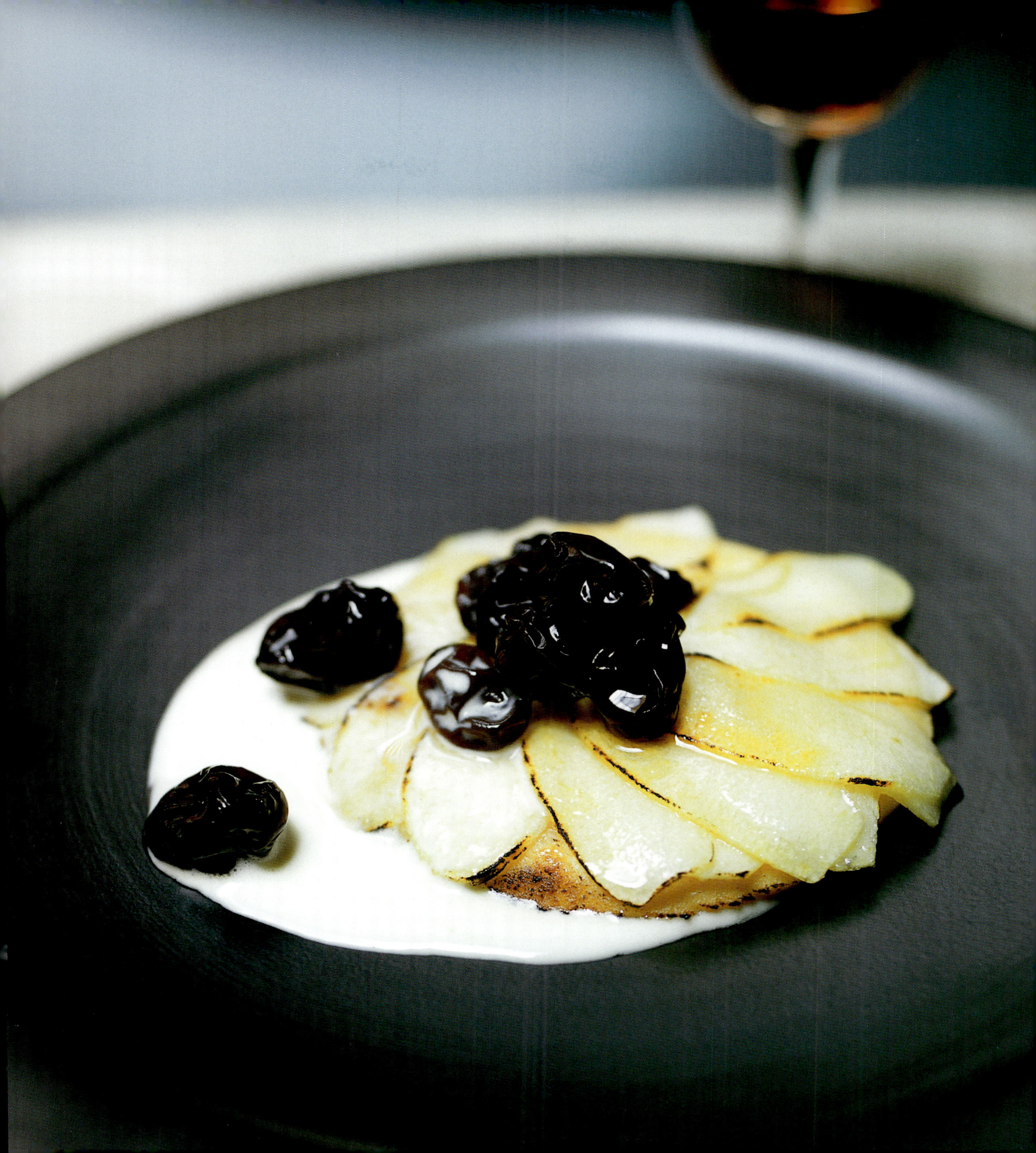

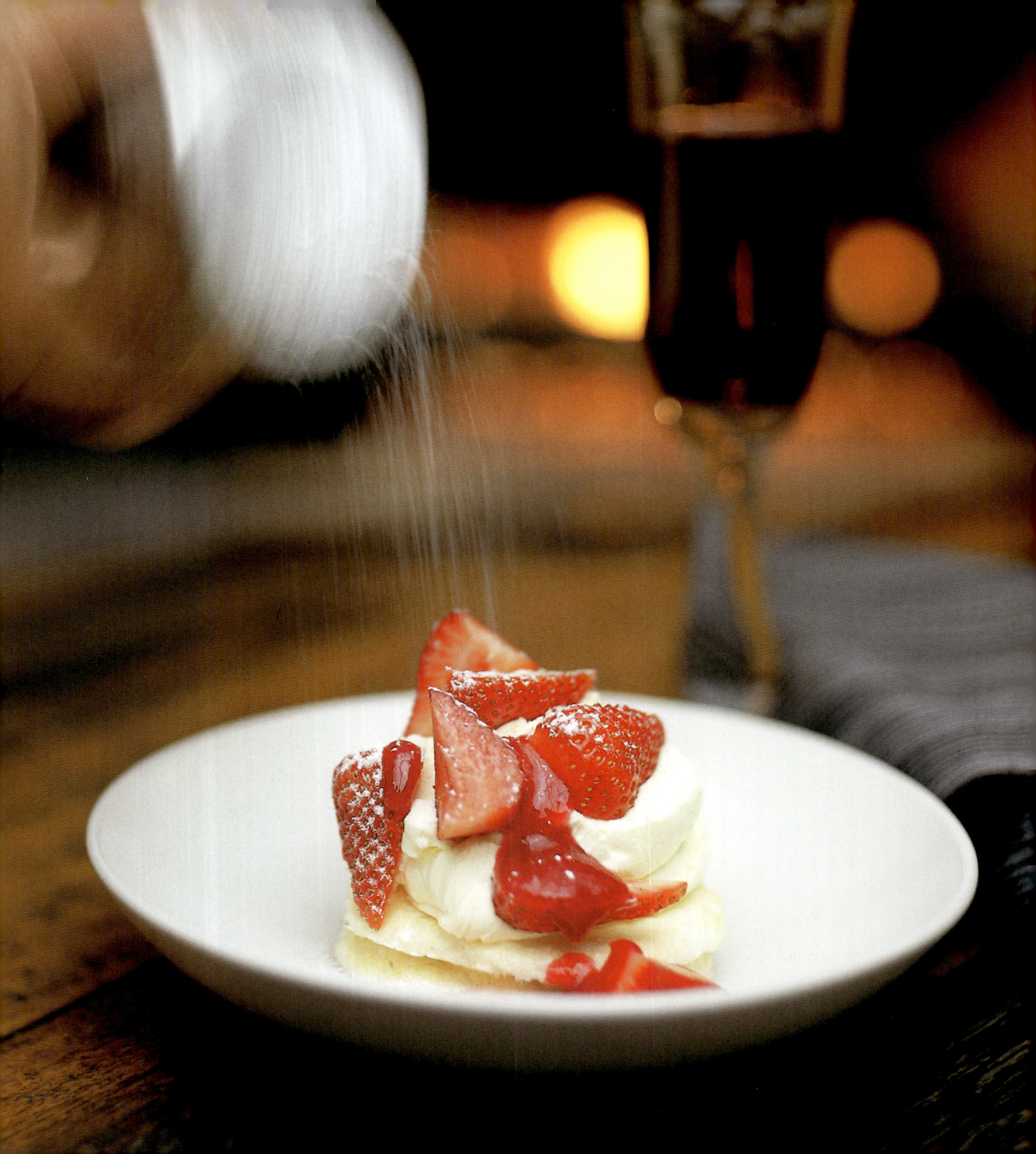

Welsh-born chef Michael James has been wowing New Zealand with his innovative food since 1991. Classically trained in Europe, Michael's food draws on the best European, Californian and Pacific Rim traditions, but with his own unique interpretation. Michael James' first restaurant, Essence, earned him a reputation as one of the country's most exciting and influential chefs. In 1999 he opened MJ's Restaurant and Bar in Auckland's vibrant Viaduct Basin.

In Auckland I am lucky enough to have local suppliers who provide me with an endless stream of good things. The end result, though, is only achieved by the enthusiasm of the people with whom I work. It was a joy to find a similar philosophy at Wyndham Estate.

Michael James

White Chocolate and Strawberry Pavlova

Meringues
6 egg whites
10 ml white balsamic vinegar
180 g caster sugar

Raspberry Coulis
60 ml caster sugar
60 ml orange juice
200 g raspberries
small squeeze lemon juice

White Chocolate Cream
200 g white chocolate
400 ml pure cream, chilled

250 g strawberries, sliced
icing sugar, to dust

Meringues
Preheat the oven to 150°C and line 2 baking sheets with baking paper. Whisk the egg whites with the vinegar until they form stiff peaks. Add the sugar, a little at a time, to make a smooth glossy meringue. Spoon the meringue into a piping bag fitted with a 1–1.5 cm plain nozzle. Pipe into 12 x 6 cm discs and bake for 45 minutes. Turn the oven off and prop the oven door slightly ajar. Leave the meringues to cool completely in the oven. Store in an airtight container until ready to serve.

Raspberry Coulis
Put the sugar and orange juice in a small heavy-based saucepan and heat gently until the sugar dissolves. Bring the syrup to the boil then lower the heat and simmer for 5 minutes. Skim away any scum from the surface, and leave to cool. Purée the raspberries in a blender then stir in the syrup and a squeeze of lemon juice.

White Chocolate Cream
To make the white chocolate cream, melt the chocolate over a bowl of hot water and cool until barely tepid. Whip the chilled cream to soft floppy peaks then fold in the white chocolate.

To Serve
Spread each meringue disc with a generous amount of white chocolate cream. Stack two discs on top of each other and top each stack with strawberries and a light dusting of icing sugar. Drizzle with raspberry coulis and serve straight away.

Serves 6

Try a sparkling white – or even a sparkling red with this dessert. The dry, fresh nature of either of these two wines will balance the sweetness of the dessert.

Liquorice Parfait with Lime Syrup

Luke Mangan

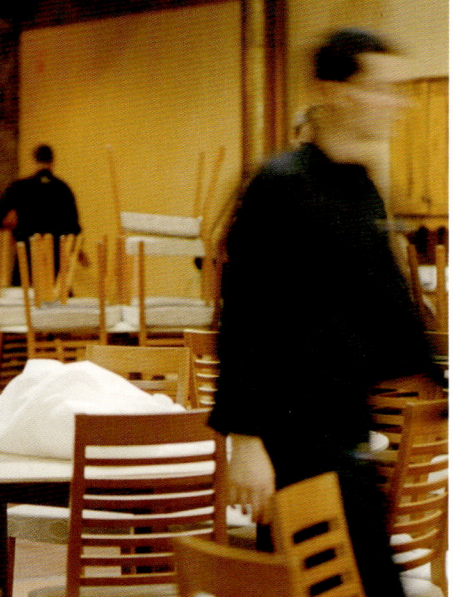

Liquorice Parfait
50 g liquorice
300 ml cream
2 eggs
1 egg yolk
60 g caster sugar
2 teaspoons liquid glucose
2 tablespoons Pernod
lime segments
  to garnish (optional)

Lime Syrup
250 g caster sugar
250 ml water
juice and finely grated zest of 1 lime

Liquorice Parfait
Place the liquorice and cream in a small saucepan and heat gently without boiling until the liquorice is very soft. Blend the mixture in a food processor until well combined, then strain through a fine sieve to remove any tiny bits of liquorice. Set aside to cool.

Put the eggs, egg yolk, sugar, glucose and Pernod in a small saucepan and set inside a larger pan of gently simmering water. Whisk to make a sabayon, until the mixture turns pale and fluffy. Remove from the heat and continue whisking as it cools a little. Fold half the sabayon into the liquorice mixture. Once combined, fold in the remaining sabayon. Pour into individual moulds or a log-shaped tin and freeze for at least 3 hours, preferably overnight.

Lime Syrup
Put the sugar and water into a heavy-based saucepan and bring to the boil, stirring to dissolve the sugar. Remove from the heat and add the lime juice and zest to taste. Stir well and leave to cool. Refrigerate until ready to serve.

To Serve
Dip the moulds briefly in hot water to loosen. Carefully ease the parfait out and place one in the centre of each dessert plate (cut into slices if you are using one long tin). Pour the lime syrup over the parfait, or serve it separately in a jug. Garnish with lime segments if using, and serve straight away.

Serves 6

Baked Mirabelle Plum Custard with Fruits in Red Vinegar Syrup and Hazelnut Biscuit

Anthony Mussara

Baked Mirabelle Plum Custard
8 egg yolks
2 whole eggs
180 g caster sugar
5 ml vanilla extract
800 ml thickened cream
240 g mirabelle plums
   or prunes that have been soaked in
   boiling water until soft, drained,
   cooled and stones removed
icing sugar for dusting

Fruits in Red Vinegar Syrup
300 ml red wine vinegar
180 ml water
240 g caster sugar
2 hard green pears, peeled, cored
   and cut into 2 cm thick slices
1 punnet blueberries
1 punnet strawberries,
   hulled and cut in half

Hazelnut Biscuit
100 g caster sugar
80 g egg whites, (about 2)
20 g plain flour
30 g ground hazelnuts
20 g melted butter

Baked Mirabelle Plum Custard

Preheat the oven to 150°C. Place the egg yolks, whole eggs, sugar and vanilla in a stainless steel bowl and whisk until thick and pale. Put the cream in a heavy-based saucepan and heat until nearly boiling. Pour the hot cream onto the egg mixture, whisking constantly.

Roughly chop the plums or prunes and place 4–5 pieces in the bottom of 8 x 140 ml dariole moulds. Place the dariole moulds in a deep ovenproof baking dish and carefully fill each one with custard. Pour hot water into the baking tray, to about halfway up the height of the moulds. Place in the oven and cook for 60–70 minutes, or until just set.

Remove from the oven and allow to cool in the water. Once cool, cover and refrigerate until required.

Fruits in Red Vinegar Syrup

Place the vinegar, water and sugar in a heavy-based stainless steel saucepan. Bring to the boil, then lower the heat to a simmer. Add the pears and cook for around 15 minutes or until tender. Lift the pears out of the syrup and reserve. Raise the heat and boil the syrup until it is reduced by half. Pour the reduced syrup over the pears. Add the blueberries and strawberries and stir gently to combine. Cover and refrigerate until ready to serve.

Hazelnut Biscuit

Preheat the oven to 170°C. Place all the ingredients in a food processor and mix until combined and smooth. Grease and line a baking tray with baking paper. Drop dessertspoons of the mixture the tray and cook for around 8 minutes, or until golden brown. Remove from the oven and lift the biscuits onto wire racks to cool. Store in an airtight container.

To Serve

Dip each of the dariole moulds in hot water for 60 seconds then unmould onto serving plates. Spoon some of the fruits on and around the custard and top each with a hazelnut biscuit. Dust with a little icing sugar and serve.

Serves 8

Conversion Tables

Volume	
millilitres	fluid ounces
25–30	1
60	2
75	2 １/２
90	3
100	3 １/２
125	4
150	5
200	7
250	8
300	10
400	13
500	16 (1 pint)
750	1 １/２ pints
1 litre	1 ３/４ pints
2 litres	3 １/４ pints

Weight	
grams	ounces
25–30	1
60	2
75	2 ２/３
80	2 ３/４
90	3
100	3 １/２
125	4
150	5
200	7
250	8 (１/２ lb)
300	10
350	12 １/３
400	14
500 (１/２ kg)	1 lb 2 oz
1 kg	2 lb 3 oz

Translations	
Beetroot	beets
Capsicum	bell pepper
Caster sugar	superfine sugar
Coriander	cilantro
Cornflour	cornstarch
Cos lettuce	romaine lettuce
Eggplant	aubergine
Icing sugar	confectioners' sugar
Plain flour	all-purpose flour
Polenta	cornmeal
Prawns	shrimp
Rocket	arugula
Snowpeas	mange tout
Spring Onions	scallions
Witlof	Belgium endive
Zucchini	courgette

Temperatures		
celsius	fahrenheit	description
120	245	very cool
140	280	
150	300	cool
160	320	warm
180	350	moderate
190	375	fairly hot
200	390	
210	410	hot
220	425	
230	450	very hot
240	475	extremely hot

Teaspoons, tablespoons and cups		
metric spoons	millilitres	fluid ounces
1 teaspoon	5	
1 tablespoon	20	
１/４ cup	60	2
１/２ cup	125	4
1 cup	250	8
4 cups	1 litre	2 pints

Note: 1 US tablespoon = 15 ml

This book uses metric cup measurements (I.e. 1 cup = 250 ml)

In the US 1 cup = 8 fl oz, while in the UK 1 cup = 10 fl oz

American and British cooks should adjust their measurements accordingly.

Directory of Guest Chefs

Sara Adey
Food, wine and tourism educator
darlingmills@ozemail.com.au

Mark Armstrong
Bistro Marlo
11–21 Wentworth Street
Manly NSW
Tel: +61 (0)2 9976 0800

Mark Best
Marque
355 Crown Street
Surry Hills NSW
Tel: +61 (0)2 9332 2225

Tony Bilson
Bilson's
27 O'Connell Street
Sydney NSW
Tel: +61 (0)2 8214 0496

Guillaume Brahimi
Guillaume at Bennelong
Sydney Opera House
Bennelong Point
Sydney NSW
Tel: +61 (0)2 9241 1999

Ian Burrows
Durham's Restaurant
2 Durham Street
Glenelg SA
Tel: +61 (0)8 8294 8224

Gavin Cleary
Nick's Seafood Restaurant
The Promenade,
Cockle Bay Wharf
Sydney NSW
Tel: +61 (0)2 9264 1212

Serge Dansereau
Bather's Pavilion
4 The Esplanade
Balmoral NSW
Tel: +61 (0)2 9969 5050

Derek Davis
Main Street Restaurants
4386 Main Street,
Philadelphia PA 19127
USA
Tel: +1 215 487 1700

Greg Doyle
Pier
594 New South Head Road
Rose Bay NSW
Tel: +61 (0)2 9327 6561

Peter Doyle
Est
Level 1, 252 George Street
Sydney NSW
Tel: +61 (0)2 9240 3010

Frank Fol
Sire Pynnock Restaurant
Hogeschoolplein 9–10
Leuven Belgium
Tel: +32 1620 2532

Peter Howard
Food and wine commentator
peterh@spiderweb.com.au

Michael James
Euro Restaurant
Shed 22,
Princes Wharf
Quay Street
Auckland NZ
Tel: +64 9 309 9866

Tony Johansson
Vamps
227 Glenmore Road
Paddington NSW
Tel: +61 (0)2 9331 1032

Cheong Liew
The Grange Restaurant
Hilton Hotel Adelaide
Victoria Square
Adelaide SA
Tel: +61 (0)8 8217 2000

Ross Lusted
Aman Resorts
Singapore
Tel: +65 6883 2555

Stefano Manfredi
Manfredi Enterprises
39–41
Lower Fort Street
The Rocks
Sydney NSW
Tel: +61 (0)2 9252 4324

Luke Mangan
Salt
229 Darlinghurst Road
Darlinghurst NSW
Tel: +61 (0)2 9332 2566

Michael Manners
Selkirks Restaurant
179 Anson Street
Orange NSW
Tel: +61 (0)2 6361 1179

Ben Moechtar
Wildfire Restaurant and Bar
Overseas Passenger Terminal
Circular Quay West
Sydney NSW
Tel: +61 (0)2 8273 1222

Matthew Moran
Aria
1 Macquarie Street
East Circular Quay
Sydney NSW
Tel: +61 (0)2 9252 2555

Anthony Musarra
radii
1 Parliament Square
East Melbourne VIC
Tel: +61 (0)3 9224 1211

Tony Papas
Allpress Espresso
58 Epsom Road
Rosebery NSW
Tel: +61 (0)2 9662 8288

Damien Pignolet
Bistro Moncur
The Woollahra Hotel
116 Queen Street
Woollahra NSW
Tel: +61 (0)2 9363 2519

Marc Polese
Mezzaluna
123 Victoria Street
Potts Point NSW
Tel: +61 (0)2 9357 1988

Ralph Potter
Café Bonton
192 The Mall
Leura NSW
Tel: +61 (0)2 4783 4377

David Rayner
Berardo's
49 Hastings Street
Noosa Heads QLD
Tel: +61 (0)7 5447 5666

Dietmar Sawyere
Forty One
Chifley Tower,
2 Chifley Square
Sydney NSW
Tel: +61 (0)2 9221 2500

Darren Simpson
Aqua Luna
Shop 18,
Opera Quays
East Circular Quay
Sydney NSW
Tel: +61 (0)2 9251 0311

Index of Chefs and Recipes

Adey, Sara 52, 58
almonds
  Candied orange rice with buttered almonds and baked rhubarb sauce 124
  Galette of almonds with clotted cream 101
  Apple galette with muscatel compote and crème anglaise 128
Armstrong, Mark 49

Baked mirabelle custard with fruits in red vinegar syrup and hazelnut biscuit 133
beef
  Roast beef tenderloin with shallot confit, Paris mash and Merlot sauce 33
  Beef brisket and beef tenderloin with mushroom confit and creamy potato 64
  Poached fillet of beef with mushroom custard and caramelised witlof 122
  Prime beef tenderloin on spinach with Vintner's butter 124
  Roast fillet of beef with baby spinach, witlof and Madeira sauce 94
  Roast fillet of beef with mushroom risotto cake and mushroom ragoût 65
  Seared Hereford tenderloin Wyndham Estate style 92
  Surf and Turf 95
beetroot
  Organic beets and smoked swordfish with landcress, dill and horseradish-crème fraîche dressing 54
  Beetroot soup with horseradish 106
  Crepinette of duck and confit duck with flageolet beans and truffle oil and beetroot purée 115
  Tartare of tuna and salmon with beetroot oil 78
Best, Mark 118, 128
Bilson, Tony 80, 101
Bitter chocolate mousse with lemon-coriander sorbet 69
Black rice and palm sugar pudding with caramelised pineapple and vanilla 73
Brahimi, Guillaume 33, 38
Bruléed rhubarb tart 39
Buffalo ricotta tart with tomatoes, pesto and caperberries 83
Burgundy cheese puffs 18
Burrows, Ian 34, 42

cakes
  Chocolate fudge cake with raspberry coulis and double cream 99
  Sauterne and olive oil cake with roasted peaches 96
  Candied orange rice with buttered almonds and baked rhubarb sauce 126
capsicum
  Roasted eggplant, bocconcini and peperonata 23
  Confit of Tasmanian salmon with a fennel, red pepper and herb slaw 52

Escalavida terrine with tapenade 107
Cauliflower and cheddar soup with gruyère parcels and chive oil 76
Celeriac remoulade with fresh crab and rocket 108
cheese
  Burgundy cheese puffs 18
  Buffalo ricotta tart with tomatoes, pesto and caperberries 83
  Cauliflower and cheddar soup with gruyère parcels and chive oil 76
  Fromage blanc tart with lime compote and nougatine 67
  Roasted eggplant, bocconcini and peperonata 23
  Rotolo of smoked salmon, lime mascarpone and salsa verde 82
chicken
  Chicken Riviera with Nicoise potatoes and fennel sauce 118
  Corn-fed spatchcock with Indonesian sweetcorn fritters and coriander pesto 58
  Roasted chicken on spring vegetable ragoût 26
  Yellow chicken curry with banana, pineapple, onion and coriander in coconut cream 86
chocolate
  Bitter chocolate mousse with lemon-coriander sorbet 69
  Chocolate and nougat tartufo 40
  Chocolate fudge cake with raspberry coulis and double cream 99
  Marmalade, ginger and chocolate pudding 98
  White chocolate and strawberry pavlova 131
Cleary, Gavin 110, 116
Confit of ocean trout with baba ghanoush and preserved lemon oil 114
Confit of Tasmanian salmon with a fennel, red pepper and herb slaw 52
Crepinette of duck and confit duck with flageolet beans and truffle oil and beetroot purée 115

Dansereau, Serge 64, 67
Davis, Derek 84, 95
desserts
  Apple galette with muscatel compote and crème anglaise 128
  Baked mirabelle custard with fruits in red vinegar syrup and hazelnut biscuit 133
  Bitter chocolate mousse with lemon-coriander sorbet 69
  Black rice and palm sugar pudding with caramelised pineapple and vanilla 73
  Bruléed rhubarb tart 39
  Candied orange rice with buttered almonds and baked rhubarb sauce 126
  Chocolate and nougat tartufo 40
  Chocolate fudge cake with raspberry coulis and double cream 99
  Fromage blanc tart with lime compote and nougatine 67

Galette of almonds with clotted cream 101
Infused poached pears with vanilla bean ice-cream 38
Liquorice parfait with lime syrup 132
Marmalade, ginger and chocolate pudding 98
Orange pot au crème, orange sorbet and orange salad 36
Panna cotta with fresh raspberries and grappa Jacopo Poli Pinot 71
Passionfruit brulée with coconut dacquoise 102
Sauterne and olive oil cake with roasted peaches 96
Sauterne jelly with fresh strawberries and honey sabayon 68
Tart sablé of roasted fruits in spiced caramel with port wine granita 42
White chocolate and strawberry pavlova 131
Deverall, Brett 82, 87
Doyle, Greg 20, 30, 36
Doyle, Peter 107, 124
dressings 20, 28, 46, 48, 52, 54, 60, 84, 90, 108, 112
duck
  Crepinette of duck and confit duck with flageolet beans and truffle oil and beetroot purée 115
  Slow-roasted duck with steamed figs, star anise and mustard fruits 89

eggplant
  Confit of ocean trout with baba ghanoush and preserved lemon oil 114
  Roasted eggplant, bocconcini and peperonata 23
  Escalavida terrine with tapenade 107
fennel
  Salad of spanner crab, shaved fennel and mustard cress with citrus vinaigrette 20
  Chicken Riviera with Nicoise potatoes and fennel sauce 118
  Confit of Tasmanian salmon with a fennel, red pepper and herb slaw 52
  Fennel-crusted guinea fowl with rosemary and figs 87
  Poached Atlantic salmon salad with tomato-fennel salsa 49
figs
  Fennel-crusted guinea fowl with rosemary and figs 87
  Slow-roasted duck with steamed figs, star anise and mustard fruits 89
fish
  Salad of smoked rainbow trout with Chardonnay dressing 48
  Confit of ocean trout with baba ghanoush and preserved lemon oil 114
  Marinated olives, semi-dried tomatoes and brandade de Morue 80
  Organic beets and smoked swordfish with landcress, dill and horseradish-crème fraîche dressing 54

Pan-fried barramundi with globe artichoke, asparagus and spinach and rich Shiraz jus 116
Striped marlin loin with cardamom sauce, spicy potatoes and peas 56
see also salmon; tuna
Fol, Frank 50, 62, 69
Fromage blanc tart with lime compote and nougatine 67
fruit
  Black rice and palm sugar pudding with caramelised pineapple and vanilla 73
  Infused poached pears with vanilla bean ice cream 38
  Olive-fried octopus with avocado and pink grapefruit salad 46
  Passionfruit brulée with coconut dacquoise 102
  Sauterne and olive oil cake with roasted peaches 96
  Tart sablé of roasted fruits in spiced caramel with port wine granita 42
see also specific fruit

Galette of almonds with clotted cream 101
game and game birds
  Fennel-crusted guinea fowl with rosemary and figs 87
  Seared venison with blackberries and pistachio-herb crust 34
George, Greg 86, 92, 99
ginger
  Marmalade, ginger and chocolate pudding 98
  Raw salmon with soy, ginger and shallot dressing 112
Grilled prawns three ways 84
Grilled Tasmanian half-shell scallops with Mediterranean salsa 110
honey
  Sauterne jelly with fresh strawberries and honey sabayon 68
  Warm honey-glazed quail on a potato galette with snowpea salad 24
Howard, Peter 48, 65

ice creams and sorbets
  Bitter chocolate mousse with lemon-coriander sorbet 69
  Chocolate and nougat tartufo 40
  Infused poached pears with vanilla bean ice cream 38
  Orange pot au crème, orange sorbet and orange salad 36
  Tart sablé of roasted fruits in spiced caramel with port wine granita 42
  Tomato salad with balsamic syrup, black pepper and green pea sorbet 50
  Infused poached pears with vanilla bean ice cream 38
James, Michael 121, 131
Johansson, Tony 18, 24, 28
lamb
  Loin of lamb with braised lentils and rosemary aïoli 90

Mignonettes of lamb with sweet roasted garlic, creamed potatoes and rosemary jus 30
Noisettes of lamb with carrot purée and a warm summer vegetable salad 62
Roast suckling 'Ilabo' lamb with rosemary and roast potatoes 31
Wild pepper-crusted lamb with Pacific gnocchi and mint gremolata 121

lemon
  Bitter chocolate mousse with lemon-coriander sorbet 69
  Confit of ocean trout with baba ghanoush and preserved lemon oil 114
Liew, Cheong 46, 73
lime
  Fromage blanc tart with lime compote and nougatine 67
  Liquorice parfait with lime syrup 132
  Rotolo of smoked salmon, lime mascarpone and salsa verde 82
  Liquorice parfait with lime syrup 132
Loin of lamb with braised lentils and rosemary aïoli 90
Lusted, Ross 89, 96

Manfredi, Stefano 23, 31, 40
Mangan, Luke 106, 112, 122, 132
Manners, Michael 22, 26, 39
Marinated olives, semi-dried tomatoes and brandade de Morue 80
Marmalade, ginger and chocolate pudding 98
Mignonettes of lamb with sweet roasted garlic, creamed potatoes and rosemary jus 30
Moechtar, Ben 83
Moran, Matthew 114
Musarra, Anthony 133
mushroom
  Beef brisket and beef tenderloin with mushroom confit and creamy potato 64
  Poached fillet of beef with mushroom custard and caramelised witlof 122
  Roast fillet of beef with mushroom risotto cake and mushroom ragoût 65
Noisettes of lamb with carrot purée and a warm summer vegetable salad 62

olives
  Escalavida terrine with tapenade 107
  Marinated olives, semi-dried tomatoes and brandade de Morue 80
  Olive-fried octopus with avocado and pink grapefruit salad 46
oranges
  Orange pot au crème, orange sorbet and orange salad 36
  Candied orange rice with buttered almonds and baked rhubarb sauce 126
Organic beets and smoked swordfish with landcress, dill and horseradish-crème fraîche dressing 54

Pan-fried barramundi with globe artichoke, asparagus and spinach and rich Shiraz jus 116
Panna cotta with fresh raspberries and grappa Jacopo Poli Pinot 71
Papas, Tony 56, 68

Passionfruit brulée with coconut dacqouise 102
peas
  Striped marlin loin with cardamom sauce, spicy potatoes and peas 56
  Tomato salad with balsamic syrup, black pepper and green pea sorbet 50
Pignolet, Damien 108, 115, 126
Poached Atlantic salmon salad with tomato-fennel salsa 49
Poached fillet of beef with mushroom custard and caramelised witlof 122
Polese, Marc 82, 87
potato
  Warm honey-glazed quail on a potato galette with snowpea salad 24
  Beef brisket and beef tenderloin with mushroom confit and creamy potato 64
  Chicken Riviera with Nicoise potatoes and fennel sauce 118
  Mignonettes of lamb with sweet roasted garlic, creamed potatoes and rosemary jus 30
  Roast beef tenderloin with shallot confit, Paris mash and Merlot sauce 33
  Roast suckling 'Ilabo' lamb with rosemary and roast potatoes 31
  Striped marlin loin with cardamom sauce, spicy potatoes and peas 56
Potter, Ralph 76, 90, 98
Prawn custard with prawn bisque 22
Prime beef tenderloin on spinach with Vintner's butter 124

quail
  Warm honey-glazed quail on a potato galette with snowpea salad 24

Raw salmon with soy, ginger and shallot dressing 112
raspberries
  Chocolate fudge cake with raspberry coulis and double cream 99
  Panna cotta with fresh raspberries and grappa Jacopo Poli Pinot 71
Rayner, David 102
rhubarb
  Bruléed rhubarb tart 39
  Candied orange rice with buttered almonds and baked rhubarb sauce 124
rice
  Black rice and palm sugar pudding with caramelised pineapple and vanilla 73
  Candied orange rice with buttered almonds and baked rhubarb sauce 124
  Roast fillet of beef with mushroom risotto cake and mushroom ragoût 65
  Roast beef tenderloin with shallot confit, Paris mash and Merlot sauce 33
  Roast fillet of beef with baby spinach, witlof and Madeira sauce 94
  Roast fillet of beef with mushroom risotto cake and mushroom ragoût 65
  Roast suckling 'Ilabo' lamb with rosemary and roast potatoes 31
  Roasted chicken on spring vegetable ragoût 26
  Roasted eggplant, bocconcini and peperonata 23

Roasted ribeye of free-range veal with garlic, coppa, rosemary, capers, parsley and mustard 60
Roast suckling 'Ilabo' lamb with rosemary and roast potatoes 31
Rotolo of smoked salmon, lime mascarpone and salsa verde 82

salads
  Celeriac remoulade with fresh crab and rocket 108
  Fennel, red pepper and herb slaw 52
  Olive-fried octopus with avocado and pink grapefruit salad 46
  Organic beets and smoked swordfish with landcress, dill and horseradish-crème fraîche dressing 54
  Poached Atlantic salmon salad with tomato-fennel salsa 49
  Salad of smoked rainbow trout with Chardonnay dressing 48
  Salad of spanner crab, shaved fennel and mustard cress with citrus vinaigrette 20
  Tomato salad with balsamic syrup, black pepper and green pea sorbet 50
  Snowpea salad 24
  Warm summer vegetable salad 62
salmon
  Confit of Tasmanian salmon with a fennel, red pepper and herb slaw 52
  Poached Atlantic salmon salad with tomato-fennel salsa 49
  Raw salmon with soy, ginger and shallot dressing 112
  Rotolo of smoked salmon, lime mascarpone and salsa verde 82
  Salmon coulibiac with dill-yoghurt dressing 28
  Tartare of tuna and salmon with beetroot oil 78
sauces 33, 34, 36, 49, 56, 71, 73, 92, 94, 95, 102, 110, 116, 118, 126
Sauterne and olive oil cake with roasted peaches 96
Sauterne jelly with fresh strawberries and honey sabayon 68
Sawyere, Dietmar 78, 94
seafood
  Celeriac remoulade with fresh crab and rocket 108
  Grilled prawns three ways 84
  Grilled Tasmanian half-shell scallops with Mediterranean salsa 110
  Olive-fried octopus with avocado and pink grapefruit salad 46
  Prawn custard with prawn bisque 22
  Salad of spanner crab, shaved fennel and mustard cress with citrus vinaigrette 20
Seared Hereford tenderloin Wyndham Estate style 92
Seared venison with blackberries and pistachio-herb crust 34
Simpson, Darren 54, 60, 71
Slow-roasted duck with steamed figs, star anise and mustard fruits 89
soups
  Beetroot soup with horseradish 106
  Cauliflower and cheddar soup with gruyère parcels and chive oil 76
spinach
  Prime beef tenderloin on spinach with Vintner's butter 124

Roast fillet of beef with baby spinach, witlof and Madeira sauce 94
Stone, Mark 83
strawberries
  Sauterne jelly with fresh strawberries and honey sabayon 68
  White chocolate and strawberry pavlova 131
Striped marlin loin with cardamom sauce, spicy potatoes and peas 56
Surf and Turf 95

Tart sablé of roasted fruits in spiced caramel with port wine granita 42
Tartare of tuna and salmon with beetroot oil 78
tarts
  Apple galette with muscatel compote and crème anglaise 128
  Bruléed rhubarb tart 39
  Buffalo ricotta tart with tomatoes, pesto and caperberries 83
  Galette of almonds with clotted cream 101
  Tart sablé of roasted fruits in spiced caramel with port wine granita 42
tomatoes
  Buffalo ricotta tart with tomatoes, pesto and caperberries 83
  Marinated olives, semi-dried tomatoes and brandade de Morue 80
  Poached Atlantic salmon salad with tomato-fennel salsa 49
  Tomato salad with balsamic syrup, black pepper and green pea sorbet 50
tuna
  Tartare of tuna and salmon with beetroot oil 78
  Surf and Turf 95

veal
  Roasted ribeye of free-range veal with garlic, coppa, rosemary, capers, parsley and mustard 60
vegetables
  Noisettes of lamb with carrot purée and a warm summer vegetable salad 62
  Roasted chicken on spring vegetable ragoût 26
  see also specific vegetables

Warm honey-glazed quail on a potato galette with snowpea salad 24
White chocolate and strawberry pavlova 131
Wild pepper-crusted lamb with Pacific gnocchi and mint gremolata 121
witlof
  Poached fillet of beef with mushroom custard and caramelised witlof 122
  Roast fillet of beef with baby spinach, witlof and Madeira sauce 94

Yellow chicken curry with banana, pineapple, onion and coriander in coconut cream 86

Acknowledgements

On behalf of Wyndham Estate, Jo Adamo and Kylie Leopold would like to thank all the people who have helped in the preparation of this book. First and foremost, thanks to the chefs who have contributed their recipes and participated in the Seasons Plate lunches over the years. Thanks too, to the guests who attended the Summer 2003 Seasons Plate lunch, for allowing themselves to be photographed.

Thanks to the following chefs and publishers for allowing us to reproduce their recipes: Cheong Liew, whose recipes for Olive-Fried Octopus with Avocado and Pink Grapefruit Salad and Black Rice and Palm Sugar Pudding with Caramelised Pineapple and Vanilla first appeared in his book *My Food*, published by Allen & Unwin (1995); Frank Fol, whose recipe for Tomato Salad with Balsamic Syrup, Black Pepper and Green Pea Sorbet first appeared in his book *De Groenten van Fol*, published by Uitgeverij Lannoo (1999); Serge Dansereau, whose recipes for Beef Brisket and Beef Tenderloin with Mushroom Confit and Creamy Potato and Fromage Blanc Tart with Lime Compote and Nougatine first appeared in his book *Food & Friends*, published by Harper Collins (1998).

Thanks to everyone at the Wyndham Estate winery for their commitment to the project. Particular thanks to chef Greg George for making the food shoot run so smoothly. Thanks also to his team, Kate Thompson, Louise Buyers, Rozena Khan and Noelene Russell.

Thanks also to the doyen of Wyndham Estate, Mr Joe Mellis, who retired this year. Joe has been a vital member of the Wyndham Estate team and responsible for the brilliant list of guest chefs we have hosted at the winery over the past 10 years. He will be sorely missed.

Adrian Lander is a gifted and creative photographer and his talent shines through on every page of the book. Thanks also to his assistant Louise Dixon and to Opel Khan who styled the food so beautifully. Thank you, too, to the design team, Klarissa Pfisterer and Hamish Freeman, who have made the book look so gorgeous.

Thanks to Michael Harden for telling the Wyndham Estate story and to Peter Bourne for his informative suggestions about matching wine with food. Assistant winemaker Kate Smith from Wyndham Estate is responsible for the terrific wine suggestions that accompany each recipe.

Finally, a big thanks to the team at Hardie Grant Publishing, in particular Keri Saines, whose clear vision for this project has created a beautiful Seasons Plate Cookbook which has exceeded all our expectations. A big thanks also to our editor Lucy Malouf - a master wordsmith – who has been a joy to work with.